ActionScript Developer's Guide to Robotlegs

ActionScript Developer's Guide to Robotlegs

Joel Hooks and Stray (Lindsey Fallow)

O'REILLY®

Beijing · Cambridge · Farnham · Köln · Sebastopol · Tokyo

ActionScript Developer's Guide to Robotlegs

by Joel Hooks and Stray (Lindsey Fallow)

Published by O'Reilly Media, Inc., 1005 Gravenstein Highway North, Sebastopol, CA 95472.

O'Reilly books may be purchased for educational, business, or sales promotional use. Online editions are also available for most titles (*http://my.safaribooksonline.com*). For more information, contact our corporate/institutional sales department: (800) 998-9938 or *corporate@oreilly.com*.

Editor: Mary Treseler

Production Editor: Jasmine Perez

Proofreader: O'Reilly Production Services

Cover Designer: Karen Montgomery

Interior Designer: David Futato

Illustrator: Robert Romano

Printing History:

August 2011:   First Edition.

ISBN: 978-1-449-30890-2

[LSI]

1312491305

Table of Contents

Preface

Robotlegs: Something a little bit special

In April 2009, Shaun Smith posted the following on his blog:

> Want a framework like PureMVC but without Singletons, Service Locators, or casting? Perhaps one with Dependency Injection and Automatic Mediator Registration?

> Well, you might enjoy RobotLegs AS3: yet another lightweight micro-architecture for Rich Internet Applications.

> It's got the bits that I like about PureMVC (Mediators, Commands and Proxies) without any of the bits that I'm not so fond of (Service Locator, Singletons, casting casting casting!)

Over the following six months, Shaun's Robotlegs concept gradually picked up support, gathered momentum, and through the collective efforts of a group of people who had never met in person, Robotlegs 1.0 was born.

Open source development is well understood in our community. But we shouldn't take it for granted. I (Stray) was working on some of the diagrams for the book on a flight back from the first ever Robotlegs team meet-up, and the man next to me started asking questions about what I was doing. When I told him I was working on a book about a project that was the collective effort of strangers from all over the world, none of whom expected to be paid, he was amazed.

Robotlegs has brought coding-joy to thousands of AS3 developers. There is something about using Robotlegs that not only solves our immediate coding problems but gives us insight into our architecture on a much deeper level. Joel and I each have many, many experiences of people sharing with us how Robotlegs has clarified concepts that were previously confusing to them. After only a short time using Robotlegs, developers tell us that they have become better programmers and architects generally.

The most rewarding part of being involved with Robotlegs has been witnessing people grow as programmers to the point where they become contributors of utilities and patches for the framework. Robotlegs owes its success not just to Shaun, Till, Robert and Joel, but to the dozens of people who got involved in the early discussions, the scores who have built utilities and extensions, the hundreds of early-adopters who have written tutorials and shared their enthusiasm with others, and the thousands of users who have put their trust in the framework and given Robotlegs a shot.

Shaun could never have dreamed that his little framework idea would grow and grow until O'Reilly commissioned a book about it. We hope this book does justice to Robotlegs, and the collective energy that has brought it into our world.

Who this book is for

ActionScript Developer's Guide to Robotlegs is for Flash, Flex and AIR application developers interested in using, or already using, the Robotlegs AS3 framework. It demonstrates and explains the core functionality of the Robotlegs framework and also explores the deeper issues in AS3 architecture generally and how developers can solve those problems in clean and flexible ways using Robotlegs.

This book also covers testing (TDD) of Robotlegs applications, and the rich example applications come with extensive tests.

Who this book is not for

This book is not for developers who are brand new to object-oriented programming. It assumes some understanding of classes, interfaces and inheritance as implemented in AS3. It is not a quick reference guide to the Robotlegs API.

Conventions used in this book

The following typographical conventions are used in this book:

Italic
> Indicates new terms, URLs, email addresses, filenames, and file extensions.

`Constant width`
> Used for program listings, as well as within paragraphs to refer to program elements such as variable or function names, databases, data types, environment variables, statements, and keywords.

`Constant width bold`
> Shows commands or other text that should be typed literally by the user.

`Constant width italic`
> Shows text that should be replaced with user-supplied values or by values determined by context.

This icon signifies a tip, suggestion, or general note.

 This icon indicates a warning or caution.

Using code examples

This book is here to help you get your job done. In general, you may use the code in this book in your programs and documentation. You do not need to contact us for permission unless you're reproducing a significant portion of the code. For example, writing a program that uses several chunks of code from this book does not require permission. Selling or distributing a CD-ROM of examples from O'Reilly books does require permission. Answering a question by citing this book and quoting example code does not require permission. Incorporating a significant amount of example code from this book into your product's documentation does require permission.

We appreciate, but do not require, attribution. An attribution usually includes the title, author, publisher, and ISBN. For example: "*ActionScript Developer's Guide to Robotlegs* by Joel Hooks and Stray (Lindsey Fallow) (O'Reilly). Copyright 2011 Newloop Ltd. and Visual Empathy LLC, 978-1-449-30890-2."

If you feel your use of code examples falls outside fair use or the permission given above, feel free to contact us at *permissions@oreilly.com*.

Safari® Books Online

 Safari Books Online is an on-demand digital library that lets you easily search over 7,500 technology and creative reference books and videos to find the answers you need quickly.

With a subscription, you can read any page and watch any video from our library online. Read books on your cell phone and mobile devices. Access new titles before they are available for print, and get exclusive access to manuscripts in development and post feedback for the authors. Copy and paste code samples, organize your favorites, download chapters, bookmark key sections, create notes, print out pages, and benefit from tons of other time-saving features.

O'Reilly Media has uploaded this book to the Safari Books Online service. To have full digital access to this book and others on similar topics from O'Reilly and other publishers, sign up for free at *http://my.safaribooksonline.com*.

How to contact us

Please address comments and questions concerning this book to the publisher:

O'Reilly Media, Inc.
1005 Gravenstein Highway North
Sebastopol, CA 95472
800-998-9938 (in the United States or Canada)
707-829-0515 (international or local)
707-829-0104 (fax)

We have a web page for this book, where we list errata, examples, and any additional information. You can access this page at:

http://www.oreilly.com/catalog/9781449308902

To comment or ask technical questions about this book, send email to:

bookquestions@oreilly.com

For more information about our books, courses, conferences, and news, see our website at *http://www.oreilly.com.*

Find us on Facebook: *http://facebook.com/oreilly*

Follow us on Twitter: *http://twitter.com/oreillymedia*

Watch us on YouTube: *http://www.youtube.com/oreillymedia*

Acknowledgments

Shaun Smith, Till Schneidereit and Robert Penner—without you there would be no Robotlegs. You rock.

We'd like to thank our tech reviewers, who contributed insights that greatly improved the book, as well as encouraging us over the finish line: Simon Bailey, Angela Relle, Sean Moore, Doug Reynolds, Neil Manuell, Dave Hunter, Mike Cann, Weyert de Boer and James Wagstaff.

Stray says: "I need to thank my wife and family for unending support and ensuring I still ate, drank and slept while working on this book. And the amazing twitter AS3 community who boost me regularly with their love for Robotlegs. And Joel for sharing this opportunity with me and tolerating my bossiness."

Joel says: "Kristina, Cree, Haze, Tripp and Cyan—thanks for putting up with me!"

A huge thank you to Rich Tretola, Meghan Blanchette, Mary Treseler and all at O'Reilly who made this book possible.

CHAPTER 1

Robotlegs is a lightweight framework for ActionScript 3

By *lightweight* we mean that it's a handy pocket knife that can get a lot of jobs done, not a complete toolkit that can attend to every eventuality. Robotlegs has a very focussed scope—facilitating the relationships between the objects in your application.

By *framework* we mean that it provides a skeleton for your application. The majority of your code will be specific to your project, but underneath that unique body sits a set of bones which are broadly the same each time. These bones allow the different parts of your application to function as a coherent system.

What does Robotlegs actually do?

The term *framework* is used very loosely in our community, referring to anything from *The Flex Framework* to jQuery or Ruby on Rails. The definition of a framework is simply:

> A reusable set of libraries or classes for a software system.

This doesn't really tell you much at all about what any particular framework does and doesn't do.

Robotlegs is a communication-and-cooperation framework

In an AS3 application, objects can communicate and cooperate in two different ways:

Direct conversation

One object has a direct reference to another object, and it calls its API (its public methods) to communicate and cooperate with it.

Passing messages

In AS3, this takes the form of the event system. One object can listen for a message, in the form of an `Event`, on another object. Typically this means that the listening is done directly, but it doesn't have to be—the display list or a shared reference to an `IEventDispatcher` can allow this to be done in a more loosely coupled way (meaning that the objects don't directly have to know about each other).

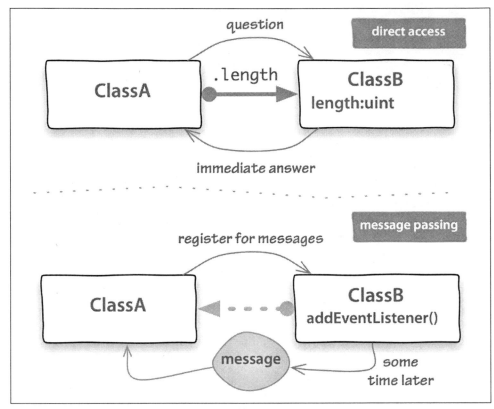

Figure 1-1. Direct conversation vs passing messages between objects

Robotlegs helps with direct conversations and message passing

Robotlegs helps make both of these forms of communication and cooperation easier to set up, meaning that you can spend more time focussed on the individual pieces of your app—which are usually the interesting and unique parts—and less time focussed on how you're going to connect them together.

Robotlegs makes use of three object-oriented architectural patterns

Automated Dependency Injection
> Providing objects with their dependencies (other objects they need to use) instead of the objects creating or fetching their own dependencies.

The Command Pattern
> Encapsulating individual pieces of application logic inside dedicated objects instead of spreading all of that logic through a single controller class.

The Mediator Pattern
> Using a dedicated object as a mailman/woman to facilitate communication between different objects, instead of those objects talking directly to each other.

If these are new to you, don't worry; we'll cover them in plenty of detail in this book. Even if you're familiar with them, you may find that the Robotlegs implementation varies a little from how you've used them in the past; solution patterns don't dictate code, they describe an *approach* to a common problem.

Do you need a framework at all?

Before you can choose the right framework for your project, you should really consider whether you need to use a framework at all. Many great programmers argue against using frameworks—the main objection being that given a shiny 'Golden Hammer', everything looks like a nail. On the Robotlegs help forum, one of the most common responses we give to newcomer questions is, "You really don't need to use the framework to do that." Here are some of the significant pros and cons of frameworks in general, as we see them:

Table 1-1. The pros and (balancing) cons of using frameworks

Pros	Cons
Consistency	Framework learning curve
Common understanding brings easier collaboration	Terminology confusion
Peer-reviewed solutions	Performance tradeoffs
A well-tested skeleton	Framework coupling
Less code to write	'Black box' code is hard to debug

Reasons to use a framework

Consistency

Frameworks encourage you to take the same approach to similar problems each time you solve them. This reduces the 'cognitive overhead' you carry for your architecture, because you only have to think about the parts that are unique and interesting.

Common understanding brings easier collaboration

If you need to bring in additional coders on your project, they should be able to follow your codebase if they have an understanding of the framework. Someone who is familiar with Robotlegs will quickly feel at home in any Robotlegs project.

Peer-reviewed solutions

The back-and-forth between the contributors to an open-source framework encourages the honing of good solutions that are flexible enough to solve a range of problems for different programmers. This flexibility also benefits your application.

A well-tested skeleton

Assuming your chosen framework comes with a full set of unit tests (and it should), you can be confident that it behaves as intended. Be aware that tested never equals perfect, but with good test coverage it should be possible to fix bugs that are found without breaking functionality. The tests are also a concise guide to the expected behavior of each class in the framework.

Less code to write

Frameworks generally allow you to swap a large quantity of complex code for a smaller amount of simpler 'boilerplate' code. (This shouldn't be your primary motivation for picking a framework, as writing code is only a small fraction of how we spend our time.)

Reasons not to use a framework

Framework learning curve

You have to learn to translate your problems to the solutions that the framework authors favored. This means changing your coding and architecture behavior, which requires you to do some brain rewiring. That's not trivial when you're trying to solve problems that are unique to your application at the same time.

Terminology confusion

Words are significantly more effective than just pointing and grunting, but where you don't share the framework's exact definition of a term, you can suffer from increased cognitive overhead; "That's not what I would have meant by mediator".

Performance tradeoffs

Code that is flexible is rarely as fast in execution as code that is finely tuned to solve one specific problem.

Framework coupling

You may find that you're unable to reuse your code in projects which don't use the same framework.

'Black box' code is hard to debug

When you're using third party utilities, including frameworks, it's hard to be confident about whether bugs are being caused by your own custom code, by the way you're using the framework or by a problem with the framework itself.

Robotlegs aims to amp up the pros and minimize the cons

The Robotlegs originators had used other frameworks in the past, and were really conscious of the potential pitfalls when they set out to create Robotlegs, so you should find less of the downside when using Robotlegs than you might normally find when adopting a new framework.

Less boilerplate code is a good thing...

...but Robotlegs is not just about less code

When you ask someone why they first chose to use a framework to build their code, their first response may well be that it allowed them to build the same application with 'less code'. In particular, we value not having to write the same-old long-hand boilerplate code (code that is repeated throughout your codebase without much purpose) over and over.

```
// you have to specify all 5 parameters just to get access to weak listeners
something.addEventListener(MouseEvent.CLICK, clickMovesMenu, false, 0, true);
```

Less boilerplate is certainly one of the benefits of using a framework, but it's worth bearing in mind that the amount of time we spend actually writing code is pretty small. We spend the majority of our time thinking about the code we're writing. If there are productivity gains to be made in reducing word count, there surely must be bigger gains in reducing 'thought count'.

So, while Robotlegs does pay close attention to the amount of boilerplate required, we hope you'll experience greater benefits in your brain than your fingers.

CHAPTER 2

The Robotlegs dream...

Some great frameworks exist, but they're intimidating

When Robotlegs came into existence, there was no lack of AS3 frameworks to choose from. PureMVC and Cairngorm had forged the way. Parsley, Swiz, Mate—they were all getting plenty of attention. So why bother creating yet another AS3 framework? And what would Robotlegs offer that other frameworks didn't already have covered?

Well, that's simple—Shaun Smith was intrigued by the idea of a framework that wouldn't give him a headache—a framework that did *less*, and thus required you to learn less, change your programming behavior less and left fewer opportunities for the only metric that we think matters: *WTFs per minute*.

80% of the problems can be solved with 20% of the API

(and 90% less cognitive load)

Developers often get excited about the Robotlegs filesize footprint—adding less than 20k to your published swf. We're much more excited about the Robotlegs cognitive footprint—how little there is to learn to get up and running with Robotlegs.

Robotlegs was always intended to be a pareto* solution: it's the 20% of functionality that solves 80% of your programming problems. The YAGNIator (YAGNI = you aren't gonna need it!) was applied ruthlessly. This means that you can carry it in your brain's pocket: complete use of the core Robotlegs framework only requires you to understand how to use eight classes. Yes, eight. That's all. And these aren't monolithic enormous classes. Most Robotlegs apps require you to make use of less than twenty methods within the framework. And Robotlegs incorporates only two custom metadata tags and, in practice, most applications only ever require the use of the [Inject] tag. More on those metadata tags later.

---

* Pareto Analysis is a decision making technique which works on the principle that 80% of a set of problems can be attributed to 20% of problem-causing factors. The Pareto principle also says that you can generate 80% of the benefit by doing the first 20% of the work.

We'll cover the Robotlegs API in depth but quite slowly through the following chapters. We want to help you understand why you would choose to use a particular combination of Robotlegs classes and API to solve a problem, and what the alternative approaches might be. But in case you're craving a concrete answer to the "What is Robotlegs?" question, here's a snapshot of the most frequently used Robotlegs code in action:

Table 2-1. A taster of the most frequently used parts of the Robotlegs API

Class	Most used API functions
Context	`new VideoLibraryContext(rootView, true);` `startup();`
Command	`execute();` `dispatch(event);`
CommandMap	`mapEvent(ConfigEvent.LOAD_COMPLETE, ApplyUserSettingsCommand, ConfigEvent);`
MediatorMap	`mapView(DocumentTabMenu, DocumentTabMenuMediator);`

Mediator	`onRegister();`
	`addViewListener(TabEvent.TAB_SELECTED, dispatchDocumentFocusChange);`
	`addContextListener(QuitEvent.QUIT_REQUESTED, hilightUnsavedDocumentTabs);`
	`dispatch(event);`

EventMap	`mapListener(view.yesBtn, MouseEvent.CLICK, dispatchYes, MouseEvent);`
Actor	`dispatch(event);`

Injector	`mapValue(IUserConfig, loadedUserConfigVO);`
	`mapSingleton(UserXMLLoadingService);`
	`mapSingletonOf(IUserLoadingService, UserXMLLoadingService);`
	`mapClass(IPermissionRules, StrictPermissionRules);`
	`instantiate(DatabaseKey);`
	`getInstance(ILoggingService);`

Coding for Robotlegs shouldn't tie you to the framework

Your classes can play outside Robotlegs too!

One of the potential drawbacks of using a framework is the difficulty of reusing your classes outside of that framework. Robotlegs is, by design, minimally intrusive—for example, if you create a model or service class that is used within a Robotlegs application, you should be able to re-use that class in a non-Robotlegs application by simply providing it with one ActionScript native property: an instance of IEventDispatcher.

Robotlegs commands only require you to provide an execute() method. There are no special messaging objects, just your own custom AS3 Events (or Signals if you prefer them and use the AS3Signals extension packages).

In addition, the metadata-based Automated Dependency Injection (not nearly as fancy as it sounds, we'll de-mystify that in Chapter 4), that wires up Robotlegs applications, supports normal coding practices. Outside of Robotlegs you'll have to wire your objects together manually, but we set a very low hurdle to jump when reusing sections of your code in projects where you're integrating with another framework, or decide to go framework-free for optimization purposes.

Robotlegs aims to enable and not dictate

From the outset, Robotlegs was intended to be easy to customize. To facilitate this, instead of being a single unit, Robotlegs is separated into three layers:

The Injector
> Creates objects (using Automated Dependency Injection).

The Robotlegs Core Architecture
> Provides control flow and communication between the different tiers of your application (business logic and user interface for example).

Top Level Architecture
> Supports the individual tiers of your application. The out-of-the-box version supports *MVCS*.

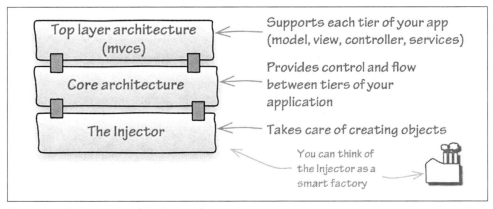

Figure 2-1. Robotlegs is a three-layer cake

The middle layer of this three-layer cake is the part that is the essence of Robotlegs. Initially the assumption was that many users would want to swap out the top and bottom layers to suit themselves.

As a result, there are very few things that Robotlegs won't 'let' you do. It's possible to implement a whole range of different patterns and architectures through Robotlegs, but we've actually found that newcomers tend to prefer a strong prescription. We often answer "Can I do X?" questions on the forum with "Yes, you *can*, but really you'd probably rather do Y". People seem to appreciate the clarity of direction.

So, while you could apply many different top-layer architectures within Robotlegs, the vast majority of users are content with the out-of-the-box architecture—what we like to think of as the standard issue *trousers* for Robotlegs. These trousers are an implementation of the architectural pattern most frequently applied to ActionScript applications: MVCS (Model, View, Controller, Service).

Most AS3 applications benefit from the MVCS approach

Model, View, Controller, Service is a pattern, which separates your application's responsibilities in a way that fits a wide range of applications.

Model
> Holds and manipulates the application's state.

View
> Relates to stuff you can see. And—confusingly—stuff you can hear too.

Controller
> Deals with application logic—translating user actions into application state changes and so on.

Service
> Links the application to external players—data services, external APIs, the user's file system etc.

Untangling MVCS in ActionScript applications

Flash, Flex and AIR applications don't always make it obvious how to untangle these parts of your application. We build components which not only render on the screen but also take decisions about whether input is valid. Are they views or controllers?

In Robotlegs, the controller layer is not intended to hold view logic—we believe that view logic belongs in the view layer (though that doesn't imply that it should live in the view class itself!). As to whether checking an email address is valid is view logic or application logic, there's no fixed answer. A good filter is that if only the view classes care about this logic, it belongs in your view layer. If other parts of the application might need to be checked or informed, it's controller code.

Testing, testing! (We test, and we make it easy for you to test)

The team behind Robotlegs is test crazy, and this has a big influence on the way Robotlegs is put together. No statics, no singletons, no reliance on display-list event bubbling. In creating Robotlegs, every single decision was subjected to the "How do I test a class that uses this?" filter.

Robotlegs makes it easy to unit test your individual classes, but it also makes it easy to integration-test features, and to end-to-end test user stories in your application.

If you're already a test nut yourself, you'll appreciate the reduction in setup that nicely decoupled cooperation and communication gives you. If you've dabbled in testing but found yourself smacking into walls relating to difficulties testing your classes in isolation, you should find that working with Robotlegs removes those problems completely. Again, the consistent approach that a strong framework gives you means that, once you've learned the ropes, you only have to apply real brain power to what's unique and interesting about each part of the code when you test it.

If you're not sold on testing, or you've never given it a try, we strongly recommend that you experiment with incorporating it into your workflow. Test-first development is hard—it's hard because it forward-shifts your confusion. You can't fiddle with your code while you ignore the fact that you haven't really figured out what this class is meant to do, or how it's going to fit in with the other classes in your application. We've found that testing is like a really (horribly) honest friend. It frequently tells you things you really didn't want to hear right now. It's up to you whether you listen!

⌇ ⌇ The Robotlegs Way

How to get every last drop of Robotlegs goodness

While Robotlegs is intended to be flexible, don't confuse that with 'anything goes'.

The folk behind Robotlegs have a great deal of respect for the wisdom of the developers that forged the way in object-oriented programming, identifying patterns and best practices that they felt were valuable and transferable, and then sharing that experience so generously.

Discussions around coding best practices can get heated, but the Robotlegs forum is a space where there's a lot of good quality and flame-free back-and-forth about good and better ways to solve specific problems. We understand that most projects are under time pressure, but we also believe that good practices and patterns largely emerge out of pain and crisis. They're not constructed on paper; they're the product of heuristic learning, of people repeatedly bashing their heads on the same problem until they find a way to stop a particular pain.

Robotlegs is powerful. It can quickly turn good code into a great application and can, just as quickly, turn bad code into a knotted mess. So, as well as 'how', we'll also cover some 'what' and 'why'—attempting to offer guidelines that will guarantee you don't run into trouble, while also calling out the implications of breaking these guidelines so that you're able to weigh up the pros and cons of taking shortcuts.

⌇ ⌇

Some final things every Robotlegs cadet should know

None of your normal AS3 OO solutions stop being relevant just because you're using Robotlegs. Well, almost none—there are two significant exceptions:

- Static Singletons. No more `static public function getInstance()`
- Event bubbling through the display-list (you can still bubble mouse events within composite views, but you won't need to rely on bubbling for wiring your application together)

As your codebase becomes more flexible, you'll start to notice higher-order problems that previously never bothered you because they were obscured by more immediate difficulties. This happens to all of us. It is a great problem to have—so try to enjoy pushing through it, shifting your architectural skills to the next level, and remember to:

- Favor composition over inheritance—composing the functionality of a class out of smaller classes is more flexible than imposing long inheritance chains, and Robotlegs makes composition very easy to do

- Make use of factories and helpers to keep each class adhering to the *Single Responsibility Principle*—every class should have one job and do it well

Robotlegs is not a Golden Hammer. Not every problem in your codebase is a nail. Specifically, Robotlegs should stay out of your views. There is an understandable temptation to use Robotlegs and Automated Dependency Injection everywhere—resist! Resist!

CHAPTER 3

Anatomy of a Robotlegs application

We're not going to bother with any Robotlegs *HelloWorld*, or even *HelloTwitter*—the truth is that Robotlegs only makes sense when applied to a real project. So most of the code samples in this book refer to two real personal projects by the authors. They're small enough not to overwhelm a first time Robotlegs user, but they're meaty enough to expose some of the problems and complexities that Robotlegs really excels at dealing with.

Rather than walk through the whole applications, we'll pull out specific features and show how they're implemented in isolation and how they connect to the wider application.

You'll find the complete source for these projects, including tests, at *https://examples .oreilly.com/9781449308902-files*.

Obviously we weren't able to cover every aspect of the framework in these two applications—particularly where we wanted to show how *not* to do things—so there are also some code snippets and examples that sit in isolation. These snippets are generic enough to make sense without having to understand the application they sit within. To differentiate between code you'll find in the demos and code that's just a snippet, we've prefixed code from our demo applications with KanbanApp: and MosaicTool: before the source filename in the code sample title.

Joel's Personal Kanban

Without going into too much detail about Kanban, it is literally translated to English from Japanese as 'signboard'. Developed by Toyota as a lean manufacturing process, Kanban has been adopted in software development as a way to track work in progress. Figure 3-1 shows a simple Personal Kanban application that allows you to create cards and track their status.

This application isn't complete, feature rich, or polished. It is a minimal viable implementation of the idea of a Personal Kanban that you can expand on easily following the patterns and practices you learn in this book.

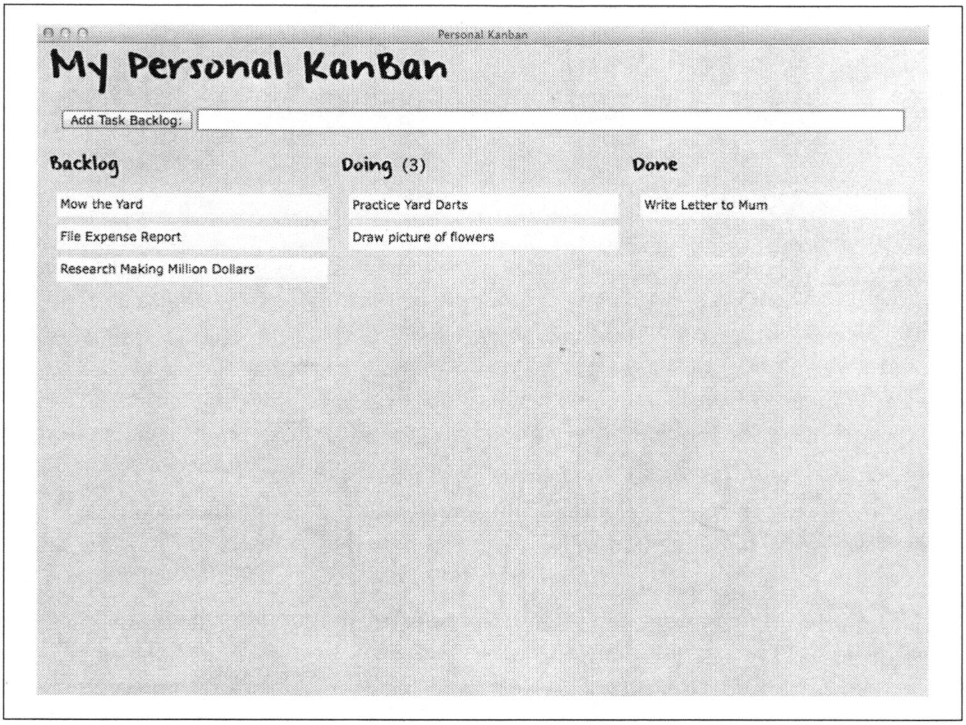

Figure 3-1. Personal Kanban Tool Screenshot

Requirements:

- Adobe AIR, Flex 4
- The user has access to three 'lanes':
  —Backlog
  —Doing
  —Done
- The user creates cards that represent tasks and gives them a title (required) and a description (optional)
- Tasks are automatically added to the 'backlog lane'
- When ready to work on a task, the user moves (drags) the relevant card into the 'doing lane'
- The 'doing lane' has a limit to the number of cards that can be added to it

---

- The user can delete items
- When a task is completed, the user moves the card to the 'done lane'
- Additional features (not implemented in our demos but you could implement them as an exercise)
  —Customized lanes
  —The user can adjust the 'doing lane' limit
  —Tracking important times for cards (created, added to doing, completed—etc.)
  —Change card color

Lindz's Mosaic Design Tool

I decided to create a large and complex square tile mosaic on an outside wall at our house in Spain. I imagined something mostly based on geometric patterns but with a pair of lizards hidden in the design. I was a bit naive at the outset, not realising how many revisions to the design I'd need to do. Coloring pencils and squared paper quickly became super-frustrating, which led me to build the design tool shown in Figure 3-2.

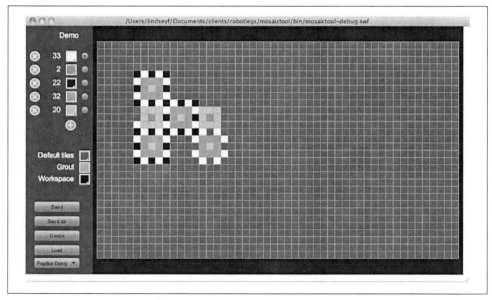

Figure 3-2. Mosaic Design Tool

Requirements:

- Swf/Standalone exe/projector, AS3 + Flash Assets
- The tool allows the user to create a grid of a known size (rows x columns)
- The user can add 'supplies' of tiles in different hex colors

- The user selects a tile color and then clicks a square on the grid to assign it this color
- The software keeps count of how many of each tile are used
- The user can save and load their designs via a local shared object (SOL)
- The user can change the color of default tiles
- The user can change the color of the grout lines
- The user can change the color of the workspace
- Additional features (not implemented in our demos but you could implement them as an exercise)
  - The user can print the design
  - The user can double-click a square to split it into four triangular tiles (across the diagonals)
  - The user can assign colors to the quarter tiles in the same way as whole tiles
  - Double-clicking a quarter tile restores the whole tile to this color
  - The user can add extra rows and columns mid-way through the design
  - The user can copy and paste a section of the design

How a Robotlegs application gets things done

Although every Robotlegs application solves a unique problem, the ways in which the objects solving that problem cooperate and communicate are consistent. The tiers of the application—models, views, controllers and services—mostly communicate through a shared eventDispatcher. We'll look at each layer in more detail later, but for now, a good place to start is with an overview of how the layers come together.

Architecture begins with Events and Commands

When you're setting out to build your first Robotlegs application, you'll probably wonder where to begin. Of course, views are always satisfying, and clients like to get their hands on something they can see, but the real lever you can pull when architecting a Robotlegs application is the controller layer: Events and Commands.

Assuming you have a collection of user stories, as we do with the Kanban and Mosaic apps, you can translate these stories into pseudo-architectural 'WHEN-THEN' statements, like "WHEN the user clicks a tile THEN the tile will change color."

These WHEN-THEN statements allow you to begin to work out what the events that will drive your application are likely to be, what action takes place, and whether that action involves the model, service or view layers. It also gives you an early lead on the actions in your application which are likely to require the most complex responses. Out of this insight you can begin to form your architectural design.

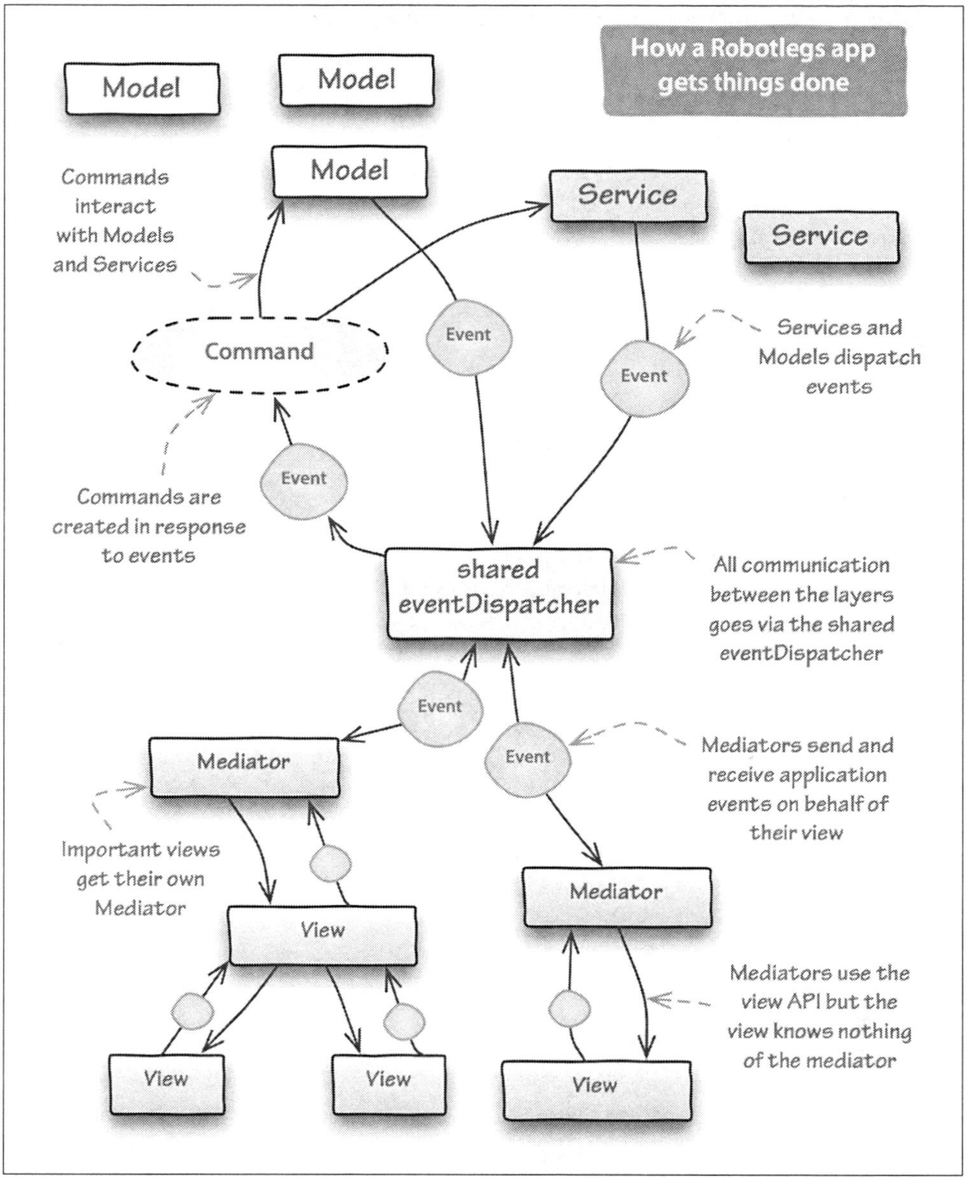
How a Robotlegs app gets things done
Model
Model
Model
Service
Service
Commands interact with Models and Services
Command
Event
Event
Services and Models dispatch events
Event
Commands are created in response to events
shared eventDispatcher
All communication between the layers goes via the shared eventDispatcher
Event
Event
Mediator
Mediators send and receive application events on behalf of their view
Important views get their own Mediator
View
Mediator
Mediators use the view API but the view knows nothing of the mediator
View
View
View

Figure 3-3. An overview of how a Robotlegs application gets things done

Table 3-1. WHEN-THEN statements for the Mosaic Tool (excerpt)

Statement	Source	Interested parties
WHEN the user clicks the save button THEN the design is saved	View (save button)	Design model, Saving service
WHEN the user changes the workspace color THEN the change is shown AND remembered	View (workspace color selector)	Workspace view, Configuration (preferences) model, Configuration saving service
WHEN the user changes the default tile color THEN the view updates	View (default color selector)	Design model, Grid view
WHEN the user changes the color of a tile THEN the count updates	View (tile in mosaic grid)	Tile counts model, Tile supply view (with counter)

The 'WHEN' parts of these statements usually become events, and the 'THEN' parts either become commands (actions on models and services) or they become view API functions, called by the view mediators. The interested parties start to give you hints about the kinds of Models and Services your application is likely to need.

It's likely that you already use a process like WHEN-THEN, but it has probably become so automatic that you don't realise you're doing it. As with any major change to your workflow, introducing Robotlegs into your applications might disturb that automatic process, so engaging in it deliberately is a good tool for finding your architectural feet.

The controller packages alone from our two demo applications will tell you a lot about how those user-stories translated, via WHEN-THEN statements, into Robotlegs-flavored MVCS. If you've got the source at hand, have a quick look at the file listings of our controller packages (don't worry about looking at the code, just the contents of the folders). If you don't have them at hand, here's a selection. See if you can spot which ones correspond to the WHEN-THEN examples above:

- Commands in the Mosaic Tool
    — ApplyConfigWorkspaceColorCommand.as
    — ChangeDefaultTileColorCommand.as
    — ChangeTileSupplyColorCommand.as
    — ChangeWorkspaceColorCommand.as
    — CombineTileSupplyCommand.as
    — CreateDesignColorsCommand.as
    — LoadConfigCommand.as
    — LoadDesignCommand.as
    — NewDesignCommand.as
    — RefreshDesignColorsCommand.as
    — SaveConfigCommand.as
    — SaveDesignCommand.as

- —SelectTileSupplyCommand.as
- —UpdateDesignCommand.as
- Commands in the Personal Kanban
  - —DatabaseErrorHandlerCommand.as
  - —DeleteTaskCommand.as
  - —LoadStatusesCommand.as
  - —LoadTasksCommand.as
  - —SaveTaskCommand.as
  - —UpdateTaskWithStatusCommand.as

You might have spotted one glaring hole in the 'how Robotlegs gets things done' story so far: configuration. It's all very well *you* knowing that WHEN a certain event happens THEN you want the application to respond in a particular way—but how do you express that in your Robotlegs app? And how does Robotlegs link these Models and Services and Views together?

Getting to grips with Robotlegs architecture

Remember the list of eight classes with their less-than-twenty key API methods? Those classes are the bones of your Robotlegs application, some of them may have sounded familiar, others might have sounded quite foreign. To build a Robotlegs application, you'll need to get to know all of the following:

- Context—used for configuration
- Actor—extended by Models and Services
- MediatorMap—used to wire Views to Mediators
- Mediator—used to wire Views to the eventDispatcher
- EventMap—used to manage event-listener relationships
- CommandMap—used to wire Events to Commands
- Commands—used to do work on Models and Services
- Injector—a smart-factory for Dependency Injection

The 'context' is the heart of your Robotlegs application

The Robotlegs *context* is the starting point for your application's configuration. In a small application, it might contain all your configuration. In a larger application, it just does enough to get the ball rolling, and the details of configuration might be delegated to a number of other classes (usually commands).

The Context class has one very important method: startup()

Robotlegs tries to use unambiguous terminology for classes and functions, but the *context* is perhaps the least obvious bit of jargon in the toolkit. The term 'context' makes most sense when you imagine reusing a class or interface in different applications.

You could then say things like:

- "In *this context*, `AppEvent.QUIT` triggers the `SaveBeforeQuittingCommand`, but in *that context*, `AppEvent.QUIT` triggers the `OfferToSaveChangesCommand`."
- "In *this context*, the `IUserDataSavingService` is fulfilled by the `UserSharedObjectSavingService`, where as in *that context* the `IUserDataSavingService` is fulfilled by the `UserRemoteXMLSavingService`".

See?

Your models and services are 'Actors' in your app

Models and services in a Robotlegs application share a base class we call `Actor`. This allows them to send events to the application to keep it informed of changes in state and progress or errors.

The MediatorMap provides a way to join your views to your app layer

In Robotlegs, your views are essentially islands, totally separated from your main application. The mediator map allows you to provide views with their own personal bridge to, and from, the rest of the application. Whenever a view lands on the stage, Robotlegs will check to see whether you have requested a mediator for this view—if you have, it'll be created and they'll be automatically paired up.

Robotlegs mediators are bridges, not view controllers

Mediators are *not* your view layer. They will likely be placed in your view package, because it's lovely to be able to see instantly which views have mediators, and the mediator needs access to the view's API, so internal package-access is appropriate. But the mediator is a bridge. It is a connector with a very narrow intended scope: minimal connection between the view and the application. Don't imagine it as part of your view layer—adding view logic to mediators gets messy very quickly. Just use your mediator to translate application events into actions on the view API, and view-events into application events, and you'll stay out of trouble.

The CommandMap makes things happen

You use the `CommandMap` to 'map' events to one or more commands, which should be executed when the event specified occurs. A command is just a class which has a public `execute()` method. You typically use commands to interact with your models and services.

The shared event dispatcher joins everything together

All of this becomes a coherent system through the Robotlegs shared event dispatcher. A `Context` creates a single instance of an `IEventDispatcher`, which is then provided to every model, service, mediator, command, and used by the command map too.

... and it goes a little something like this (event flow)

When a model dispatches an update event on this shared event dispatcher, you can pick this up in a view's mediator and pass the data to the correct view.

Then, when a user clicks a button on the view, the mediator can pick up this action, turn it into a custom event relevant to the application, and dispatch this event on the shared event dispatcher.

The command map can then pick up this event and trigger the command that was mapped to it. And other mediators for relevant views can get in on the action as well.

Your classes stay loosely coupled—generally coupled only to the specific custom events they are interested in—and yet you can efficiently pass data and action requests around the whole application.

User stories as implemented in Robotlegs

There are plenty of code-based examples coming up, but to give you a picture of how we bring the different parts of our application together, here are some descriptive walk-throughs of specific user-stories in each application. If you're desperate to get into the code, you can always dive into the source and try to seek out the lines of code that correspond to each step in the process.

Personal Kanban example: Moving a task from 'backlog' to 'doing'

The Kanban saves the user's status continually, so every action has to be captured in the external storage—in this case a local database. If you have ever implemented something like this, it would be worth recalling the solution, or solutions, you've used, so you can compare them with the Robotlegs solution.

1. The 'doing' TaskLane dispatches an UpdateTaskWithStatusEvent for the dragged task, and the 'doing' status
2. The TaskLane mediator redispatches this to the whole application
3. The UpdateTaskWithStatusCommand is triggered
4. This command updates the task to the 'doing' status
5. The command then dispatches a SaveTaskEvent for this task
6. The SaveTaskCommand is triggered

7. The SaveTaskCommand checks the status of the task, and provided it's valid, then asks the TaskService to save the task

8. The TaskService saves the task

Mosaic Design Tool example: Saving a design

The Mosaic tool only saves the design when the user requests it. In this case the storage is a local shared object. Again, if you've ever tackled this yourself, it's worth remembering how you achieved it.

1. The SaveButtonMediator responds to the CLICK on the SaveButton by dispatching a SAVE_REQUESTED event

2. The SaveDesignCommand is triggered

3. The SaveDesignCommand pulls the current design's name from the user's config, and passes it to the DesignSavingService

4. The DesignSavingService attempts to save the design, reading it from the Design-Model

5. The DesignSavingService dispatches a SAVE_COMPLETED event

The same but different

What you might have noticed is that, although our two applications have very little in common, and although we developed them completely separately, and even though one is a Flex application and the other is a pure AS3 application, the *flow* through our applications is strikingly similar.

So, there it is—flexibility (solving very different problems) and consistency (using the same approaches) together. This is why so many people have found that Robotlegs equals coding joy.

All of this is possible because of the Robotlegs Injector

The magic (except it's not really magic, just some very neat code reflection) that makes this mix of consistency and flexibility feasible is the Robotlegs Injector. When a command is created in response to an event, the injector automatically provides the command with everything it needs to do its work—models, services, even the event that triggered it. This automagic population of the command with the instances it needs is called *Automated Dependency Injection*.

CHAPTER 4

Automated Dependency Injection

You may well have heard of *Dependency Injection*—there's a certain buzz around the term that has been moving through the ActionScript community for the last couple of years. It's one of those terms that sounds like it must be really sophisticated and complex, but actually turns out to be a fancy name for a simple concept that you already understand how to use.

This doesn't mean that it's not powerful and interesting, but, as with most design patterns, it's the neat capturing of an idea that many programmers encounter on their own into a single specific term—'Dependency Injection'—that is most useful. You were probably already doing it; now you'll have a more pithy way of referring to it.

So, what exactly is Automated Dependency Injection?

First of all, it's worth knowing that Dependency Injection—also known as DI—is a complicated name for something you've been doing since the first time you passed a parameter to a function.

A dependency is just a requirement to use another object

If the UserXMLLoader class needs to be passed a loadScriptPath:String of the url from which to load its data, this is a dependency:

```
public function UserXMLLoader( loadScriptPath:String )
```

A dependency implies configuration, cooperation or communication

If objectA needs an instance of objectB, it must be because it needs to use it for:

- Configuration: A wants to use B in a read-only style
- Cooperation: A wants to use B through its API (public methods)
- Communication: A wants to register listeners for messages dispatched by B

You can fulfil a dependency in three different ways

When an instance of one class needs to use an instance of another class, you can support this relationship (fulfil the dependency) in various ways:

1. You can create a new instance of a class within the object that is dependent on it

2. You can use the locator pattern to pull a pre-existing instance of the dependency into the class that is dependent on it. This decouples your dependent class from knowing how to construct the class it's dependent on. But of course your class is now dependent on the locator too

3. You can 'manually inject' it. Inject in this situation really just means 'create it somewhere else and give it directly to the dependent object'

You already use Dependency Injection

Any time you do any of these, you're using DI:

Constructor injection

```
public class UserXMLLoader
{
    // declares the dependency in the constructor
    public function UserXMLLoader( loadScriptPath:String )
    {
    }
}

// the dependency is fulfilled at instantiation:
var userXMLLoader:UserXMLLoader = new UserXMLLoader(remoteScriptPath);
```

Public property injection

```
public class UserXMLLoader
{
    // declares the dependency as a public property
    public var loadScriptPath:String;
}

var userXMLLoader:UserXMLLoader = new UserXMLLoader();

// dependency is fulfilled by setting a public property after instantiation:
userXMLLoader.loadScriptPath = remoteScriptPath;
```

Setter method injection

```
public class UserXMLLoader
{
    protected var _loadScriptPath:String;

    public function UserXMLLoader( )
    {
    }
```

```
    // declares the dependency through a property setter
    public function setLoadScriptPath(value:String):void
    {
        _loadScriptPath = loadScriptPath;
    }
}

// dependency is fulfilled by setting a protected property after instantiation
// via a setter method:
var userXMLLoader:UserXMLLoader = new UserXMLLoader();
userXMLLoader.setLoadScriptPath(remoteScriptPath);
```

There are different ways to inject dependencies

So, if we're all doing DI already, why the buzz about it? The truth is that injecting dependencies is trivial in a small example, but quickly becomes tiresome in a large application—tending to result in a lot of 'pass the parcel' code where objects are holding on to properties they're not really interested in, simply so that they can 'inject' them into other objects they create or interact with.

Configuration, cooperation and communication related dependencies are key to the responsibilities of the class—you could say that these are 'real' dependencies. Pass the parcel dependencies could be said to be 'artificial' dependencies. If objectA needs to use objectB, and objectB requires objectC for configuration, this imposes an artificial dependency (on C) on objectA.

This particular problem is the one we're usually seeking to avoid when we resort to using statics and globals as property holders in our code, or use an object locator pattern. Solving dependency-chain problems in this way is really just a case of shuffling the problem from place to place, sacrificing something in return for each solution.

Statics and globals make code rigid, brittle, hard to test, and prone to memory leaks

Static properties and methods have their place—nobody would argue that a function that finds prime factors isn't a good use of static—but when we use statics to hold state we make big sacrifices in other areas. We can easily use a static value to configure the UserXMLLoader, but now it's hard to test how the class responds to connection failures or bad responses from the script. We also couple the UserXMLLoader to the AppConfig —when really it only wants to know about the script path.

```
public class UserXMLLoader
{
    protected var _loadScriptPath:String;

    public function UserXMLLoader()
    {
        // pulls the dependency through a static reference
        _loadScriptPath = AppConfig.loadScriptPath;
```

```
        }
}

public class AppConfig
{
    public static const loadScriptPath:String = 'http://sample.com/userXML.php';
}
```

Locator patterns push extra responsibilities on your classes

Even if you avoid using a static instance for the object that can supply your classes with
what they need, it's still a big imposition on a class to require it to do not just its job
but also know how to get all the things it needs to do its job.

It's tempting to imagine that we can 'just' use a common base class to quickly roll this
functionality into many classes across our codebase and keep it maintained in one place,
but this is a really bad place to make inheritance decisions from! And what about in-
evitable common super/subclasses that don't need this functionality but are part of the
inheritance chain?

Surely there has to be a better way?

Automated DI gets around the need to 'pass the parcel', but keeps code flexible

The intention behind automated DI containers is to abstract the fulfilment of dependencies from the application itself. Essentially, we split this job out completely, so that
the application code no longer has to do it, and instead we ask a third party—the DI
container—to get it done.

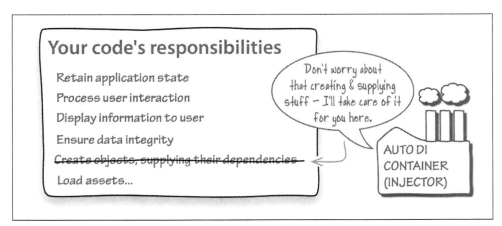

Figure 4-1. Automated DI shifts the responsibility for fulfiling dependencies to a third party

This reduction of responsibilities for your own code is a plus, but there's another advantage: being able to type your dependencies against interfaces instead of concrete types.

A `getInstance()` singleton always requires you to be dependent on a concrete class. For example, even if `UserXMLLoader` implements an `IUserLoader` interface, the `XMLUserLoadingService` has to use the actual class, and not the interface, in order to access the static `getInstance` method:

```
public class XMLUserLoadingService implements IUserLoadingService
{
    //We are stuck with the UserXMLLoader 'forever'
    private var userXMLLoader:IUserLoader = UserXMLLoader.getInstance();

    public function loadAllUsers():void
    {
        userXMLLoader.loadAll();
    }
}
```

With Robotlegs Automated DI, we can declare a particular dependency in a class, and configure our application (through our context) to know how to fulfil that dependency: which concrete class to inject against an interface for example. In this example, `IUserLoader` might be fulfilled by `XmlUserLoader`, `JsonUserLoader` or even `DummyUserLoader`:

```
public class LoadUserCommand
{
    //We can swap out our IUserLoader implementations easily.
    [Inject]
    public var userLoader:IUserLoader;

    public function execute():void
    {
        userLoader.loadAll();
    }
}
```

How does Robotlegs Injection work?

Automated DI is a handshake

Like any handshake, the Automated DI handshake has two sides:

1. The injection point in the class (asking for something to be provided)
2. The rule in the injector (defining how it should be provided)

From the developer's point of view, that's almost all there is to it. Injection point + injector rule = happy classes.

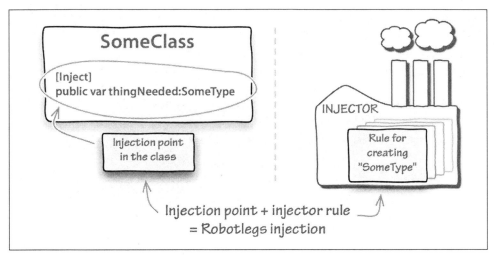

Figure 4-2. Robotlegs injection has two sides

You can specify an injection point in three ways

Injection points (dependencies that you would like to be provided) can be specified as public properties, properties with a setter function, or through your class constructor.

```
// as a public property
[Inject]
public var someProperty:IPropertyType;

... or using a setter function
[Inject]
public function setSomeProperty(value:IPropertyType):void
{
    ...
}
... or in your constructor
[Inject]
public function SomeClass(someProperty:IPropertyType):void
{
    ...
}
```

 The Automated DI container (the injector) has to be able to find out which dependencies your class would like to be injected. This means that injection points always have to be public—whether you're defining them as properties, setter functions or through the constructor. The injector will silently ignore any private or protected injection point.

And you also have to tell the injector what you would like it to do

Any injection point in your application has to be paired with a rule that you've created about how to fulfil that dependency. You do that in your context using the Robotlegs

Injector. For example, to declare a rule that anytime a class declares a dependency on IPropertyType you want to use a specific instance of UserURLParams, you'd use this:

```
injector.mapValue(IPropertyType, new UserURLParams("robotlegs.org"));
```

Limitations of custom metadata like [Inject]

If you use Flex then you're probably already familiar with metadata tagging such as [Bindable]. If you don't use Flex then this syntax may be completely new to you.

The Flash Compiler is aware of its own (native) metadata—and this metadata is mostly used at compile time in order to generate extra code that is compiled into your application. Custom metadata is different. Custom metadata isn't parsed by the Flash Compiler at all—in fact the compiler will remove it completely unless you ask it to keep it (more on that later). If you've asked your Flash Compiler to keep this metadata it will simply be included in your code—it doesn't mean anything to the compiler or to the Flash runtime.

We can find out, at runtime, what metadata a class has, and this information is what is used to power the Robotlegs Injector. Used in this way, the [Inject] tag enables something almost magical, but it's important that you understand that, unlike native metadata such as [Bindable], all custom metadata is essentially meaningless. There is nothing special about [Inject]—we could ask you to tag your injection points with [Frog] and get the same results—provided the Robotlegs Injector knew that [Frog] was the metadata to look out for.

Robotlegs has different types of injection

An injection mapping is really just a rule about how to satisfy the dependency. It's really no more complex than that. You're saying "When a class asks for this, give it this."

Robotlegs offers a choice of four rules about how the injector should respond to the request:

mapClass(SomeType, TypeA)
> Meets SomeType requests with an instance of TypeA—using a fresh instance each time (note that it injects an instance of the class, not the class itself)

mapSingleton(SomeType)
> Meets SomeType requests with the same instance of SomeType every time

mapSingletonOf(SomeType, TypeA)
> Meets SomeType requests with an instance of TypeA—using the same instance each time

mapValue(SomeType, new TypeA())
> Meets SomeType requests with the instance of TypeA provided—using the same instance each time

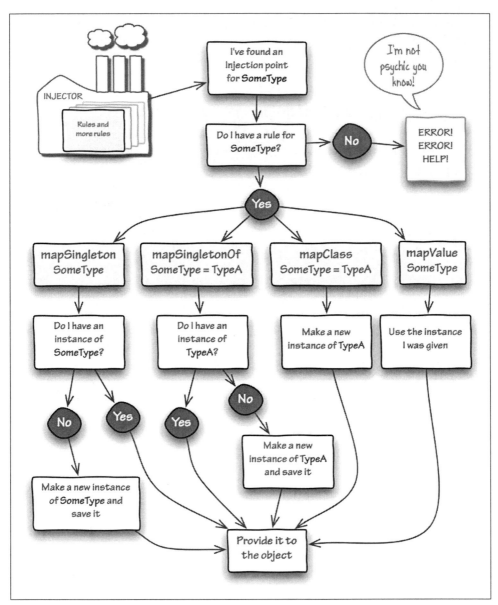

Figure 4-3. How the injector processes injection rules

If you only want one instance, use mapSingleton

```
// in the context startup();
injector.mapSingleton(UserLoadingService);
// in the class that has the dependency:
[Inject]
public var userLoadingService:UserLoadingService;
```

Unlike the getInstance() Singleton pattern, the class itself—UserLoadingService—doesn't need to know that it's going to be used as a 'singleton'—meaning that the injector will use the same instance every single time this dependency is requested. As well as freeing the UserLoadingService from the responsibility of maintaining its 'singleness', you are also now free to create additional instances if, for some reason, you needed to.

Neat!... but our code is now coupled to the actual implementation class. Our injection points declare UserLoadingService as their dependency. We can do better!

mapSingletonOf keeps your code coupled only to interfaces

```
// in the context startup();
injector.mapSingletonOf(IUserLoadingService, UserLoadingService);
// in the class that has the dependency:
[Inject]
public var userLoadingService:IUserLoadingService;
```

Now we're free to switch the concrete UserLoadingService for a DummyUserLoadingService or LocalUserLoadingService in the context and we know that every single class that is dependent on the injected IUserLoadingService will get this kind of concrete instance instead.

⌥⌥ The Robotlegs Way

Inject against interfaces

The Robotlegs framework does!

Separating the API contract of your dependency from the actual implementation isn't just about flexibility. An interface has a smaller cognitive footprint—you can instantly feed your brain *only* the details that it needs to be interested in at that moment.

⌥⌥

What if my class has to be created elsewhere? (e.g. a factory)

mapValue lets you control the creation of the singleton instance:

```
// in the context startup();
injector.mapValue(IUserURLParams, new UserURLParams("Robotlegs.org"));
// in the class that has the dependency:
[Inject]
public var userURLParams:IUserURLParams;
```

`mapValue()` works much like `mapSingletonOf()`, except that it's your code, instead of the injector, that controls the creation of the instance that is provided to each object that has this dependency. How you create this instance is up to you, with all the usual options—`new Thing()`, factories, fluent builders*—available to you.

You can only create one rule per class

Automated Injection is limited to one rule per dependency class, in each context. (See, context is making more sense now, isn't it?)

So, this would explode, because the injector has no way of telling which value to use for which injection:

```
// in the class that has the dependencies:
[Inject]
public var url:String;

[Inject]
public var username:String;
// in the context startup();
mapValue(String, 'Robotlegs.org');
mapValue(String, 'Joel Hooks');
```

Named rules let you create multiple rules for each class (but they're icky)

The injector actually lets you map multiple injections against the same class, if you provide an additional parameter—a 'name' to tell the like injections apart.

```
// in the class that has the dependencies:
[Inject(name='weburl')]
public var url:String;

[Inject(name='username')]
public var username:String;
// in the context startup();
mapValue(String, 'Robotlegs.org', 'weburl');
mapValue(String, 'Joel Hooks', 'username');
```

We understand that this looks attractive initially. It means you can inject against base types without having to create custom classes. Which sounds like a plus, but the reliance on a `String` for identification is weak—with the possibility of runtime problems that are hard to test and debug if you accidentally use the wrong name.

```
// in the class that has the dependencies:
[Inject(name='usrname')]
public var username:String;
```

---

* A fluent builder uses a natural-language approach to building an instance with the properties you want. For example, `var quiz:Quiz = new QuizBuilder().multipleChoice.withTitle('Robotlegs jeopardy') .withQuestionSet('robotlegs.xml').build();`

You need to tell the compiler to include the injection metadata

The Flash/Flex compiler will strip out non-native metadata unless you tell it not to – this includes the [Inject] and [PostConstruct] metadata that Robotlegs needs to function correctly. Sometimes, when building an AIR application for example, the metadata will stay intact while debugging but will be stripped out when you publish your release build.

You need to tell the compiler that you want it to keep the [Inject] and [PostConstruct] metadata tags.

The Robotlegs swc includes the required compiler arguments for you, but when linking against the source you will need to add the arguments yourself, and how you need to do that depends on what you're using to compile your code:

FlashBuilder/FlexBuilder solution

In your project properties, under 'Flex Compiler', add the following to the 'Additional compiler arguments':

```
-keep-as3-metadata+=Inject -keep-as3-metadata+=PostConstruct
```

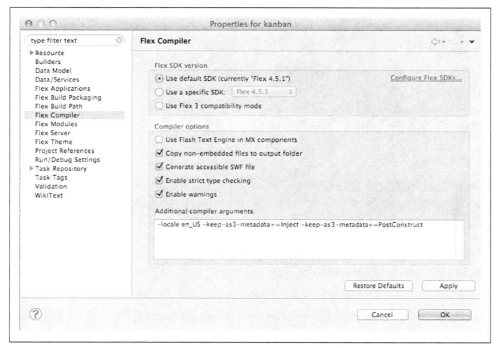

Figure 4-4. Including Robotlegs metadata in FlashBuilder

Flash CS4/CS5 IDE Solution

Flash CS4 and CS5 don't offer the option to specify the metadata arguments to the compiler directly. For a while it was thought that they couldn't be used with custom metadata at all—but it turns out that if you build against the Robotlegs swc, and you specify that you also want to build a swc of your project, the metadata stays in place. Nice!

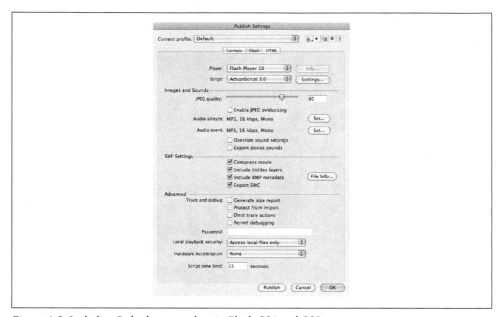

Figure 4-5. Including Robotlegs metadata in Flash CS4 and CS5

IntelliJ Solution

In IntelliJ, specific compiler arguments are provided on a per-module rather than per-project basis. In the Flex Compiler Settings for your module, in the 'Additional compiler options' add:

```
-keep-as3-metadata+=Inject -keep-as3-metadata+=PostConstruct
```

Flex SDK Solution—command line compiling

Add the following to your compiler arguments:

```
-keep-as3-metadata+=Inject -keep-as3-metadata+=PostConstruct
```

Flex SDK Solution—compiling with ant

Add the following to your compiler arguments:

```
<arg value="-keep-as3-metadata+=Inject"/>
<arg value="-keep-as3-metadata+=PostConstruct" />
```

Automated Injection 'Gotchas'

Automated DI is fairly simple once you get to grips with it, but there are a few common tripping points that can make your first experience with it frustrating if you're not aware of them.

If an object has an [Inject]ed dependency you have to create it using the Injector.

Injection isn't magic, it's just a very neat way of abstracting some factory logic when your objects are instantiated.

If you do `new ThingWithInjection()` you'll find that none of the Injections have been fulfilled. It doesn't matter where you put this code, the injector has no idea you've created a new instance and so it can't get busy injecting it. There are some tricks for manually instantiating objects with [Inject]ed dependencies in the power-ups section. In a typical implementation this won't be necessary as all your classes with Injections will be created by the Injector.

You can map injection rules at runtime, but beware of race conditions.

If your rule isn't mapped before the first time it needs to be used, you'll get an injector error.

The injection point and rule have to be of exactly the same type

The Injector allows you to specify an injection point using an interface and then fulfil it with a concrete class, but you have to make sure the first parameter in your rule matches the injection point.

This won't work:

```
// in the class file of the concrete type
public class SpecialThing implements IThing ...

// in the context
```

```
injector.mapSingletonOf(IThing, SpecialThing);

// in the class file where you declare the dependency to be injected
[Inject]
public var thing:SpecialThing    // this needed to be mapped to IThing
```

You also can't substitute superclasses/subclasses, so this won't work either:

```
// in the class file of the concrete type
public class ExtraSpecialThing extends SpecialThing ...

// in the context
injector.mapSingleton(ExtraSpecialThing);

// in the class file where you declare the dependency to be injected
[Inject]
public var thing:SpecialThing  // this needed to be mapped to ExtraSpecialThing
                               // but much better to use an interface here!
```

If you override a method that has an [Inject] tag, you need to add it in the subclass

If you extend a class with an [Inject] method and you override that method, the compiler will use the describe-type data from the subclass and not the superclass, so it won't know about the original [Inject] tag. You need to tag the subclass method with [Inject] too. If you're working on a class which includes methods with [Inject] tags that others are likely to override, give some thought to whether there's a more foolproof way to achieve the same result.

An advantage of methods over properties is that they can be declared in an interface, so if you do decide to keep your injected method for this reason, make sure you shout out the need for the [Inject] tag!

CHAPTER 5

The Robotlegs context in action

Every Robotlegs project begins with a context. Until the context is instantiated, Robotlegs isn't up and running. To get your Robotlegs application going, you have to do two things: provide the context with a contextView and ask it to run startup.

Provide the context with a root-view

Every Robotlegs application requires a root-view—an instance of DisplayObjectContainer—which is the view that will be provided to the mediatorMap, so that when child views are added to this root-view they can be automatically mediated (an instance of their mediator is created and provided with the child view that it mediates for).

 If your application is non-visual then just provide any-old placeholder instance of Sprite or DisplayObjectContainer.

Example 5-1. MosaicTool: mosaicTool.as In AS3/Flash, you'll provide this view as the first parameter of the constructor

```
public class mosaictool extends Sprite
{

    protected var _context:MosaicContext;

    public function mosaictool()
    {
        _context = new MosaicContext(this);
    }
    ...
```

Example 5-2. KanbanApp: PersonalKanban.mxml In Flex the context can be initialized with an MXML tag; not having access to the constructor, you'll provide this view using the contextView property

```
<WindowedApplication xmlns:fx="http://ns.adobe.com/mxml/2009"
                     xmlns="library://ns.adobe.com/flex/spark"
                     xmlns:kanban="robotlegs.examples.kanban.*"
                     xmlns:view="robotlegs.examples.kanban.view.*"
                     showStatusBar="false">

    <fx:Style source="css/style.css"/>

    <fx:Declarations>
        <kanban:PersonalKanbanContext contextView="{this}"/>
    </fx:Declarations>
```

Ask it to run startup()—immediately or when you're ready

In most situations you'll want to start your application as soon as possible—in AS3 this means right from the constructor, and in Flex this means as soon as the contextView has been set. This is the default, but in particular cases where you need to do something else before your context gets to work configuring and firing up your app, you can set autoStartup to false and run startup() manually.

Use startup() to provide your injection rules, map your mediators to views and commands to events

startup() is the most important method in your whole app. It's where you initially configure your application—where you determine which classes will be injected and how, which view classes will get what kind of mediators, and what commands will be triggered by events.

Example 5-3. KanbanApp: PersonalKanbanContext.as All of your application's configuration can be contained in the Context

```
override public function startup():void
{
  mediatorMap.mapView(StatusGroup, StatusGroupMediator);
  mediatorMap.mapView(TaskLane, TaskLaneMediator);
  mediatorMap.mapView(TaskEntryBar, TaskEntryBarMediator);

  injector.mapSingletonOf(IStatusService, SQLStatusService);
  injector.mapSingletonOf(ITaskService, SQLTaskService);

  injector.mapSingleton(StatusListModel);
  injector.mapSingleton(TaskListModel);

  commandMap.mapEvent(UpdateTaskWithStatusEvent.UPDATE, UpdateTaskWithStatusCommand);
  commandMap.mapEvent(SaveTaskEvent.SAVE, SaveTaskCommand);
```

```
commandMap.mapEvent(ConfigureDatabaseEvent.CONFIGURE, ConfigureDatabaseCommand);
commandMap.mapEvent(DatabaseReadyEvent.READY, LoadStatusesCommand);
commandMap.mapEvent(StatusesLoadedEvent.LOADED, LoadTasksCommand);
commandMap.mapEvent(DeleteTaskEvent.DELETE, DeleteTaskCommand);
commandMap.mapEvent(DatabaseErrorHandlerEvent.ERROR, DatabaseErrorHandlerCommand);

dispatchEvent(new ConfigureDatabaseEvent())
}
```

You will quickly find that this approach leads to a rather messy `startup()` method in an app of any significant size. In fact, the Personal Kanban example above is right on the threshold of being much too large. A solution to this is to break the configuration down into manageable chunks. The Mosaic application provides an example of doing that with configuration helper classes.

Example 5-4. MosaicTool: MosaicContext.as Breaking down configuration into small coherent helper classes

```
override public function startup():void
{
  new BootstrapConfigValues(injector);
  new BootstrapModels(injector);
  new BootstrapServices(injector);
  new BootstrapCommands(commandMap);
  new BootstrapTileSupplyCommands(commandMap);
  new BootstrapClasses(injector);
  new BootstrapViewMediators(mediatorMap);

  addRootView();
  super.startup();
}
```

Example 5-5. MosaicTool: BootstrapConfigValues.as Each bootstrap class is responsible for configuring a specific set of injections or mappings

```
public class BootstrapConfigValues
{
public function BootstrapConfigValues(injector:IInjector)
{
    injector.mapValue(ConfigName, new ConfigName("MosaicDesignerConfig"));
    injector.mapValue(DefaultDesignName, new DefaultDesignName("Practice Design"));
    injector.mapValue(DefaultGridSize, new DefaultGridSize(15, 20));
    injector.mapValue(DefaultTileColor, new DefaultTileColor(0x333333));
    injector.mapValue(DefaultWorkspaceColor, new DefaultWorkspaceColor(0x000000));
}
}
```

As your project grows you will appreciate the readability this separation of configuration concerns brings.

Shutting down a Context

In most situations you won't need to shutdown a context, but if, for example, your Robotlegs application is a game loaded into another swf, you might find it useful to be able to kill your Robotlegs context and create it again fresh when the game is restarted.

In most cases, getting rid of a context is as simple as nulling the variable where you created a reference to the context. The garbage collector will then handle all the clean up.

The Context class has a shutdown() method, which you can override if you need to do any clean up specific to your application. This should only be necessary if you've created references between your context and an object outside of it, usually in a loading shell.

If you do need to do some specific clean up, calling super.shutdown() at the end of your shutdown() method will dispatch a ContextEvent.SHUTDOWN_COMPLETE event, which you can listen for before nulling the reference to the context.

Now you have some Context

You can think of the Context as a container for the injections you specify on the injector. Within a specific Context, a set of objects are created and injected based on the configuration values setup for that Context. As well as objects and injection rules, the context contains rules about how to map views to mediators, and how to map events to commands, via the heart of your controller layer: the CommandMap.

CHAPTER 6

The CommandMap in action

Earlier in this book, we described a command as being a 'snack-sized controller'. In any meaningful application the developer has to find ways to tie the important players together—a click on a view might require a service to load some data, from which a model is updated (if there are no errors), and so on. This 'tying together' is the realm of the controller code—and it's usually the most complex and brittle code in your application. The CommandMap and the Command class exist to achieve this 'tying together' in a way that is less complex and less brittle than the typical controller approach.

A Command is a concise single-purpose controller object

The Command Pattern is a strategy for separating your controller logic into small self-contained pieces. Instead of having a monolithic MosaicController, we can separate the logic for the Mosaic application into self-describing, single-purpose classes:

Example 6-1. MosaicTool: SelectTileSupplyCommand.as

```
public class SelectTileSupplyCommand extends Command
{
    [Inject]
    public var tileSuppliesModel:ITileSuppliesModel;

    [Inject]
    public var tileSupplyEvent:TileSupplyEvent;

    override public function execute():void
    {
        tileSuppliesModel.selectedSupplyID = tileSupplyEvent.id;
    }
}
```

Commands are triggered by events

In Robotlegs, a command is usually fired in response to an Event. You specify which event you'd like to trigger which command, and then the command map waits for that event to happen and then runs the command.

Example 6-2. MosaicTool: BootstrapTileSupplyCommands.as

```
public function BootstrapTileSupplyCommands(commandMap:ICommandMap)
{
    commandMap.mapEvent(TileSupplyEvent.COLOR_CHANGED,
                        ChangeTileSupplyColorCommand, TileSupplyEvent);
    commandMap.mapEvent(TileSupplyEvent.COLOR_CHANGED,
                      RefreshDesignColorsCommand, TileSupplyEvent);
    ...
}
```

Commands can be any class with an 'execute' method

Robotlegs uses code reflection to check that your command has a public execute() method—this is the only requirement for a command that is executed through the Robotlegs command map.

There is a Robotlegs Command class in the MVCS package, which you can extend like this:

```
import org.robotlegs.mvcs.Command;

public class SomeGenericCommand extends Command
{
    public function execute():void
    {
        //do some work here
    }
}
```

But extending Command is not required. Any class with an execute() method will work fine:

```
public class SomeGenericCommand
{
    public function execute():void
    {
        //do some work here
    }
}
```

The advantage to extending the Command class is that many handy injections are already made for you. This includes access to the CommandMap, MediatorMap, and even the contextView of the current Context. Robotlegs doesn't require that you extend Command to allow for maximum flexibility within your application. The Command class is simply provided for convenience and is not required.

Commands should do their thing and then die

When the relevant event fires, the command map automatically creates an instance of each command that is mapped to it, and then runs the execute method. There's no hard reference kept to the instance of each command created, so it will die and be available for garbage collection as soon as the code triggered by its execute method has finished running.

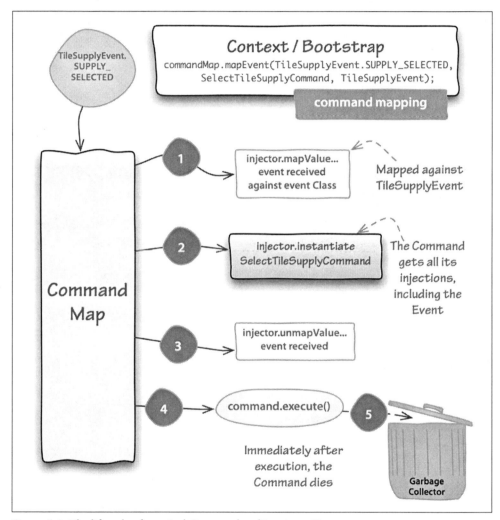

Figure 6-1. The lifecycle of a typical Command and its trigger Event

Commands rely on their injections to be useful

The most common purpose of a command is to update a model or kick off an operation on a service. Assuming that you've mapped the relevant models and services on the injector, you can just inject them into your command as required.

You can inject the event that triggered the command

As well as any class that was mapped through the injector, you can also inject the instance of the event that triggered the command. This gives you access to any properties or data that were part of the event—handy!

This event is only available for injection until the command map has finished creating the commands to be executed—then it's unmapped again, so each time a `TileSupplyEvent.SUPPLY_SELECTED` event causes the command map to create and execute a command, the most recent instance is the one that will be used.

Commands know about the injector, command map, mediator map and context view

If you extend the `Command` base class, you'll inherit injections for the `injector`, `commandMap` and `mediatorMap` properties that are used in your context, and you'll get a helper method for dispatching events:

Example 6-3. The Command class gives you access to the main Robotlegs players

```
public class Command
{
    [Inject]
    public var contextView:DisplayObjectContainer;

    [Inject]
    public var commandMap:ICommandMap;

    [Inject]
    public var eventDispatcher:IEventDispatcher;

    [Inject]
    public var injector:IInjector;

    [Inject]
    public var mediatorMap:IMediatorMap;

    public function execute():void
    {
    }

    /**
     * Dispatch helper method
```

```
    */
    protected function dispatch(event:Event):Boolean
    {
        if(eventDispatcher.hasEventListener(event.type))
            return eventDispatcher.dispatchEvent(event);
         return false;
    }
}
```

So, without specifying these injections in your own custom command, you can use the command to configure the `injector`, `commandMap` and `mediatorMap`, as well as doing work on the `contextView`.

This allows you to make and change injector mappings, command map event-command pairs and mediator map mappings at runtime.

Example 6-4. KanbanApp: In the ConfigureDatabaseCommand.as a utility class instance is mapped in the command to keep file system access isolated

```
public class ConfigureDatabaseCommand extends Command
{
    private static const DB_FILE_NAME:String = "Kanban.db";

    override public function execute():void
    {
        var dbFile:File = File.applicationStorageDirectory.resolvePath(DB_FILE_NAME);
        var sqlRunner:ISQLRunnerDelegate = new SQLRunnerDelegate(dbFile);

        injector.mapValue(ISQLRunnerDelegate, sqlRunner);

    ...
```

👢👢 The Robotlegs Way

Don't work on views in commands

Rather that using commands to do work on your views, prefer using a mediator on your context view and its child views, and API functions in the context view and child views.

If all your view-work is done through your mediator-view layer, and all your application-work is done through commands, the consistency really pays off. In fact, the MVCS setup doesn't allow an easy way to get at your views from commands. Don't try to get around this by using views as event properties if it can be avoided. Instead use that view's own mediator to listen for events that commands dispatch. 👢👢

Commands can also dispatch events

Commands have access to the shared event dispatcher, so you can use them to dispatch a new event, to be picked up in a mediator or even wired to another command—if you're using this command to check conditions and control application flow.

Great command names pay dividends

A criticism of the Command Pattern is that, compared with the more conventional 'controller' approach, the breaking up of logic into lots of individual files makes it harder to find the code you're looking for. This is only the case if you choose not to name your commands descriptively or accurately enough. Take a peek inside the command packages of the example apps—you'd probably know where to go to find the code you were interested in:

Example 6-5. MosaicTool: Well-named commands don't result in confusion

```
+-commands/
| +-AddTileSupplyCommand.as
| +-ApplyConfigWorkspaceColorCommand.as
| +-ChangeDefaultTileColorCommand.as
| +-ChangeGroutColorCommand.as
| +-ChangeTileSupplyColorCommand.as
| +-ChangeWorkspaceColorCommand.as
| +-CombineTileSupplyCommand.as
| +-CreateConfigCommand.as
| +-CreateDesignColorsCommand.as
| +-LoadConfigCommand.as
| +-LoadDesignCommand.as
| +-NewDesignCommand.as
| +-RefreshDesignColorsCommand.as
| +-RemoveTileSupplyCommand.as
| +-RequestLoadFirstDesignCommand.as
| +-RestoreGridStatusCommand.as
| +-SaveConfigCommand.as
| +-SaveDesignCommand.as
| +-SelectTileSupplyCommand.as
| +-UpdateCurrentDesignOnConfigCommand.as
| +-UpdateDesignCommand.as
```

Named and constructed well, your command package contents describe every significant 'gesture' in your application.

Naming command classes well is tricky. If you can't think of a perfect name instantly, err on the side of long-and-descriptive rather than short-and-obscure. You will probably remember to come back and rename `CheckUserHasAWorkingAccountOnTheServerCommand` to something more succinct later, but `CheckUserCommand` might never be refactored to a more descriptive name.

Use helper classes for shared logic

Another criticism of commands is that they're harder to keep DRY (don't repeat your-self) than controllers. If you find yourself repeating logic in different commands just do what you'd normally do—identify common code and put it into a shared base class, or (better) split it into a helper that you can use in both commands.

Don't over-dry your code though—it's easy to confuse coincidental 'same code' for meaningful 'same purpose'. If these two parts of code would *always* change together in future, dry it up with inheritance or composition. But if they would likely change separately in future, don't get too hooked up in avoiding duplication.

Commands make team development easier

Another advantage of using commands to break your application logic into individual actions is that you and your teammates can more easily develop individual features in isolation. Controller classes frequently lead to merge-headaches when you try to resolve conflicting changes. Commands result in fewer merge problems, and also make it easier to distinguish between 'same purpose' repeated code and incidental re-peated code.

Detain and release when you need your command to hang around

Most commands are short-lived, but occasionally you may want to keep your command alive to handle a response from an asynchronous service call and then take action based on the result. Of course you can achieve the same result by hooking up further com-mands to events dispatched by the service call, but sometimes this will require you to store some data that has been created locally in the command—which can get messy.

Don't rely on event handlers or callbacks to keep your command alive, instead be explicit and use the CommandMap's detain and release functionality to make it clear what your intention is.

Example 6-6. Relying on a callback to ensure the command isn't garbage collected, hides your intent in the implementation details

```
override public function execute():void
{
    loadingService.load(parseLoadedXML);
}

override public function parseLoadedXML(dataLoaded:XML):void
{
    var updateVO:UserData = parser.parseData(dataLoaded);
    dispatch(new UserEvent(UserEvent.USER_LOADED, updateVO));
}
```

Example 6-7. Using commandMap.detain and commandMap.release makes it clear that your intent is to use the command asynchronously

```
override public function execute():void
{
    commandMap.detain(this);
    loadingService.load(parseLoadedXML);
}

override public function parseLoadedXML(dataLoaded:XML):void
{
    var updateVO:UserData = parser.parseData(dataLoaded);
    dispatch(new UserEvent(UserEvent.USER_LOADED, updateVO));
    commandMap.release(this);
}
```

CHAPTER 7

Models and services: How are they different?

You might have heard of MVC and wondered why the S was added for the Robotlegs MVCS architecture. Why separate models from services when they both deal with data most of the time?

Models and services are very similar, but understanding their important differences can help you to use them more effectively. By separating models from services, we provide a clear line in the sand for our classes—boxing off the functionality that they should contain. A service doesn't store data. A model doesn't communicate with the outside world to retrieve data. Still—they are closely related. A model is empty without the appropriate service, and a service has no purpose without the models.

Models and Services usually extend Actor

Actor is a very simple base class—just a dependency on the eventDispatcher (a property of Actor) that is shared throughout the application. This allows your models and services to dispatch state and status updates that the whole application can pick up.

It is important to understand that you do not *need* to extend Actor. Actor is provided for your convenience, to give you the core functionality that is commonly needed by models and services in a Robotlegs application. If your models and services don't need that core functionality, or you would like them to be reused in a non-Robotlegs code base, you can provide the functionality of Actor manually without extending anything.

They don't listen, they only talk

Models and services are like the worst kind of dinner party guest. They have no interest in what other people have to say. All they do is send messages out to the framework—

they never listen directly to their eventDispatcher property to see what other classes are saying.

Use your API through a Command

Models and services expose an API (ideally one you've paired to an interface), and this is what you use to update the state of a model, ask it for data, and call methods on your services.

Distinguishing Models from Services

In pure code terms, models and services are identical in Robotlegs. The purpose of separating them into packages is to help you and the future coder on your project (which might be you as well) to understand the architecture of your application.

Mostly you'll find it's pretty obvious whether a class is a model or a service, but in ambiguous cases we find this question to be a useful sieve:

Does your class dispatch state/status update events:

1. Only synchronously, immediately following a call on its API—in which case it's a model

2. Asynchronously (usually initially triggered by a call on its API but perhaps sometime later)—in which case it's a service

The most common 'model or service?' example that crops up on the Robotlegs forum is the case of a timer used by the application. As this will dispatch events asynchronously the sieve determines that it's a service, even though it might hold some state.

Classes that don't dispatch events to the shared event dispatcher don't need to extend Actor

If your model or service isn't going to need to dispatch events to the rest of the application then you don't need to extend the Actor base class at all. For example, a model that holds configuration information, mapped as a singleton, and used by multiple services to pick up URLs and so on, doesn't need to extend Actor as it will never dispatch an event.

Non-dispatching services are rarer, usually if your service doesn't dispatch events then either you've given the service a lot of responsibility to work with other classes directly, or you're ignoring the possibility of failures and errors.

A valid non-dispatching service might be one that acts as an internal timer, and updates an injected model, or models, which then dispatch events for themselves—for example in a timer-driven game. Whether this is truly a service is hard to say—and probably not important as long as you've given it a good name—but, taking this example, the reason for avoiding the Event->Command step would be to improve performance—so the service *could* dispatch events in its own time if you wanted to use it that way.

Configuring services

If your service makes contact with the outside world, or has configurable settings, you can separate the specific values from the service by handing the configuration to the service instead of creating it internally.

This is particularly useful for spoofing situations where something has gone wrong— a lost connection, server error, security error, the script returns something you weren't expecting—really knowing how your service deals with these things is important.

Configuring services using a command

The Personal Kanban tool uses an AIR SQLLite Database to store the application data. The database has to be created using the DatabaseCreator, which in turn requires an ISQLRunnerDelegate—a wrapper to provide an interface for the native SQLRunner which unfortunately doesn't implement an interface itself.

The SQLRunnerDelegate has to be provided with a file reference for the database, which has to be resolved to use the applicationStorageDirectory. This is the kind of configuration that can seem complex when it's done by a controller which is also managing other objects. We enjoy the reduction in complexity that comes from wrapping it up as a single-purpose action in a command.

Example 7-1. KanbanApp: ConfigureDatabaseCommand.as configures the SQLite database that is used by the application

```
public class ConfigureDatabaseCommand extends Command
{
private static const DB_FILE_NAME:String = "Kanban.db";

override public function execute():void
{
    var dbFile:File = File.applicationStorageDirectory.resolvePath(DB_FILE_NAME);

    var sqlRunner:ISQLRunnerDelegate = new SQLRunnerDelegate(dbFile);

    injector.mapValue(ISQLRunnerDelegate, sqlRunner);

    if (!dbFile.exists)
    {
        // We use the injector to instantiate the DatabaseCreator here because
        // we want to inject the SQLRunner that is mapped above. This works
        // well even though the DatabaseCreator is not a mapped object, we still
        // get access to injections from Robotlegs by creating it this way!
        var creator:DatabaseCreator = injector.instantiate(DatabaseCreator);
        creator.createDatabaseStructure();
```

```
    }
    else
    {
        dispatch(new DatabaseReadyEvent());
    }
}
}
```

You probably noticed a static! Don't worry—the static constant in this command is private—it's static and constant because it will never change, not to allow other objects to access it. To test failed scenarios you would provide the DatabaseCreator with a different instance of ISQLRunnerDelegate which you had manually provided with a different database path. Or you might use a 'stub' object—more on testing your services in chapter 10.

Configuring services by injecting the configuration

If your service only needs to access configuration details such as the load path it should use and how frequently it should perform remote calls, you don't need to do this via a command and can simply inject the configuration into the service directly.

Example 7-2. You can inject a configuration class that implements an interface

```
public class RemoteLoggingService implements ILoggingService
{
    [Inject]
    public var loggingConfig:ILoggingConfig;

    public function startLogging():void
    {
        _batchInterval = loggingConfig.interval;
        _serverPath = loggingConfig.serverPath;
    }
    ...
```

Working with non-Actor models and services (including third party code)

Sometimes you'll want to work with a service or model that you didn't write, and that doesn't extend Actor. Or perhaps you have a model that contains logic but no state, and so it doesn't really make sense for it to dispatch its own events, and yet you still need the rest of the application to know about the changes it makes. There are two ways of working with classes that don't have the framework's shared event dispatcher in Robotlegs: wrap them in an Actor or use a command to dispatch events on their behalf.

Wrap them in an Actor

If you make the non-actor model or service a property of a class that extends Actor, you can use the wrapping Actor to dispatch events. This approach also allows you to implement an interface of your own choosing, which isolates your code from any changes to the API of this class in the future, so it's particularly suited to third party code.

Example 7-3. Use an Actor to wrap third party libraries

```
public class TwitterServiceWrapper extends Actor implements ITwitterService
{
protected var _remoteService:SomeTwitterService;

public function TwitterServiceWrapper(service:SomeTwitterService)
{
    _remoteService = service;
}

public function attemptLogin(username:String, password:String):void
{
    _remoteService.addEventListener(IOErrorEvent.IO_ERROR, dispatchIOError);
    _remoteService.addEventListener(TwitterEvent.OVER_CAPACITY, dispatchOverCapacity);
    _remoteService.openAccount(username, password);
}

public function dispatchIOError(e:IOErrorEvent):void
{
    dispatch(
        new TwitterServiceErrorEvent(TwitterServiceErrorEvent.IO_ERROR, e.msg));
}

public function dispatchOverCapacity(e:TwitterEvent):void
{
    var errorMessage:String = "Oh noes! Fail whale :(";
    dispatch(
        new TwitterServiceErrorEvent(TwitterServiceErrorEvent.FAIL_WHALE, errorMessage));
}
}
```

Use the command that acts upon them to dispatch the events

Work directly with the model or service in your commands, and use the command to dispatch update and status events on the shared event dispatcher. When working with asynchronous services this means you'll need to use the detain and release features of the CommandMap class to ensure your command isn't garbage collected while it's waiting.

Example 7-4. MosaicTool: RefreshDesignColorsCommand.as accesses properties in two models and passes them through a utility before dispatching an event with the combined results

```
public class RefreshDesignColorsCommand extends Command
{
    [Inject]
    public var tileSupplies:ITileSuppliesModel;
```

```
[Inject]
public var designModel:IMosaicDesignModel;

[Inject]
public var designToColorsTranslator:IDesignToColorsTranslator;

[Inject]
public var specModel:IMosaicSpecModel;

override public function execute():void
{
    var designGrid:Vector.<Vector.<uint>> = designModel.getDesign();

    var defaultTileColor:uint = specModel.defaultTileColor;
    var supplyList:Vector.<TileSupplyVO> = tileSupplies.supplyList;

    var processedDesign:Vector.<Vector.<uint>>;
    processedDesign = designToColorsTranslator.processDesign(designGrid, supplyList,
                                                             defaultTileColor);

    dispatchDesign(processedDesign);
}

protected function dispatchDesign(design:Vector.<Vector.<uint>>):void
{
    var evt:DesignEvent = new DesignEvent(DesignEvent.DESIGN_COLORS_CHANGED, design);
    dispatch(evt);
}

}
```

 Generally we prefer the 'wrap in an actor' approach because it allows you to create an interface which better matches your coding style through the rest of your codebase, particularly useful if this is code from an external library that you have little influence on.

Model design tips for Robotlegs

It's easy to be distracted by the visual parts of our application and pay much less attention to how we structure our models. This is unfortunate because your model is your opportunity to untangle the problem your application attempts to solve. How you design your model dictates how easy or difficult it is to adapt or add features to your application, as well as how much time you spend scratching your head trying to avoid tangled code.

So, your model is *really* important. In most cases it's much, much more important than your services. Don't repeat this within hearing distance of a service, but generally they're pretty dull. Move some data from here to here... whatever. For that reason, you should always let your model design drive your service design, and never the other way around.

Your model is probably also the most unique aspect of your application. It's what makes the Personal Kanban app most different from the Mosaic Tool—their views are an expression of how different the models are, but the model is what varied first. Because of this, it's hard for us to give you specific tips on how to design the models to express your own unique problem, but we do have some good general guidelines that will steer you in the right direction.

Keep those responsibilities separated

A common query on the Robotlegs forum is whether it's necessary to have one giant model that holds all of the application state. No! Definitely not! You should split your application state storage and manipulation up according to responsibilities—you can map many models, so there's no need to shove everything into one monster-model.

Use strong-typed wrappers for collections

You can't (please, please don't use named injection to get around this) inject base types such as `Array`, `ArrayCollection` or `Vector`.

If you've got a list of data items, the easiest way to work with them is to place them in a strongly-typed wrapper class that either gives you direct access to the collection or—where appropriate—includes some helpers for working with them.

Example 7-5. MosaicTool: DesignNamesList.as wraps a vector of strings and provides a convenient API to access them; while this isn't injected in the example, it easily could be—unlike a vector or other base collection

```
public class DesignNamesList
{
    protected var _items:Vector.<String>;
    protected var _selectedItem:String;

    public function DesignNamesList(items:Vector.<String>)
    {
        _items = items;
        if (_items.length > 0)
        {
            _selectedItem = _items[0];
        }
    }

    public function selectAndAddIfNeeded(item:String):Boolean
    {
        _selectedItem = item;
        if (!contains(item))
        {
            _items.push(item);
```

```
            return true;
    }
        return false;
    }

    public function get selectedItem():String
    {
        return _selectedItem;
    }

    public function get designNames():Vector.<String>
    {
        return _items;
    }

    public function get hasItems():Boolean
    {
        return (_items && _items.length > 0);
    }

    public function contains(searchFor:String):Boolean
    {
        return (_items.indexOf(searchFor) != -1);
    }
}
```

Never create mutually dependent models

ModelA injects ModelB, and ModelB injects ModelA: uh oh! This is a strong sign that you've got a design flaw. In many cases your code will blow up the first time either of these models is used (when the injector tries to instantiate and fulfil the injections and gets itself in a knot). Even if your code doesn't actually explode, there's usually a better solution, often involving a parent model that uses both of these models independently.

Managing the relationships between models and services

In many situations the purpose of your service is to load and send data for a model.

The obvious approach is to inject the model (against an interface) into the service, and have the service deal with updating the model itself, but we think this often asks the service to take on two responsibilities.

One approach is to feed the output from a service into a factory or processor, which then converts the raw data into AS3 native objects, and handles the creation and updating of the models.

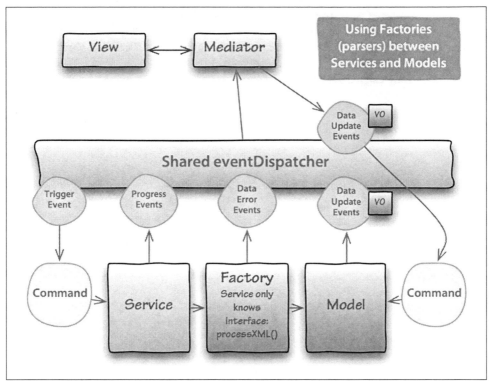

Figure 7-1. The service-factory-model relationship gives you more flexibility

Example 7-6. MosaicTool: DesignSolSavingService.as has an IDesignToDataParser injected to manipulate data and keep the service out of the data manipulation business

```
public class DesignSolSavingService extends BaseSolSavingService
{
    [Inject]
    public var designToDataParser:IDesignToDataParser;

    public function saveDesign(designName:String):void
    {
        save(designName);
    }

    // the save method in the superclass calls this method
    override protected function copyData():void
    {
        var solData:Object = _sol.data;
        solData.date = new Date();
        designToDataParser.populateDataFromDesign(solData);
    }
    ...
}
```

Separating the parser from the actual service also allows us to vary the parser and the service independently. When the model changes (perhaps we'll add a 'notes' field to the designs) we can update the parser without touching the code that connects to the local `SharedObject`. Or, if we need to load our data from a remote service providing JSON instead, we can pass the object created from the JSON direct to this parser. Neat.

CHAPTER 8

Connecting views with Mediators

What brings the 'rich' to our rich internet applications? The beautiful, animated, interactive, lovingly crafted view components that users interact with. These view components and screens can be created in any number of ways. They might be complex Flex components or pure ActionScript using low level graphics APIs. No matter how your views are developed they will need to communicate both with other views and with the services and models we discussed in chapter 7.

This is where `Mediators` come in. `Mediators` are lightweight classes that create a bridge between your view tier and the rest of your application. Mediators act as switchboards. They listen for important events that the view needs to respond to, and dispatch events to let the rest of the application know when something changes in your view—usually because of user interaction.

Introducing the MediatorMap

As with other managed objects, we need to tell Robotlegs which views connect to which mediators. This process is accomplished by using the MediatorMap. The MediatorMap is a core object that is created for you by the `Context`. Lets take a look at how the MediatorMap works.

Wiring views with the MediatorMap

The MediatorMap is available by the time the `Context` runs the startup() method. It is also available in commands that extend the Robotlegs `Command` class, or you can inject it (as `IMediatorMap`) into your own commands. In the most simple applications we will map our views within the `startup()` method in the `Context`. In more complex applications we will want to avoid this by separating out the configuration into commands.

Example 8-1. KanbanApp: Mapping mediators to views in startup()

```
public class PersonalKanbanContext extends Context
{
    override public function startup():void
    {
        mediatorMap.mapView(StatusGroup, StatusGroupMediator);
        mediatorMap.mapView(TaskLane, TaskLaneMediator);
        mediatorMap.mapView(TaskEntryBar, TaskEntryBarMediator);

        ...
    }
}
```

These views are now ready to send and receive application messages through their mediators when they are added to the stage.

 If you use the MediatorMap to map the contextView (generally your main application class) the mediator for this view will be mapped and created immediately.

Mediating your view components

Mediators act as bridges between your view components and the rest of your application. They allow your view components to exist without the burden of business logic and domain logic that is better handled by other tiers of your application. Mediators should be lightweight and carry minimal dependencies while keeping to their narrow focus of acting as a bridge.

Mediators are created when your view hits the stage

The MediatorMap listens for Event.ADDED_TO_STAGE and Event.REMOVED_FROM_STAGE on the DisplayObjectContainer you provided as the contextView. Every time a DisplayObject is added or removed, the mediator map checks whether it needs to create or destroy an associated mediator, based on the mediator map mappings you've made.

Mediator Structure

Mediators are simple by design. As shown below, your mediators declare injections, register events to listen to, and define methods to handle those events.

Example 8-2. MosaicTool: GridViewMediator.as listens for events on its view and from the Context

```
public class GridViewMediator extends Mediator
{
[Inject]
public var view:GridView;

override public function onRegister():void
```

```
{
    addViewListener(TileColorChangeEvent.CHANGED,
                        dispatch, TileColorChangeEvent);
    addContextListener(TileSupplyEvent.SUPPLY_SELECTED,
                        changeSelectionColor, TileSupplyEvent);
    addContextListener(TileSupplyEvent.SELECTED_SUPPLY_COLOR_CHANGED,
                        changeSelectionColor, TileSupplyEvent);
    addContextListener(GroutEvent.COLOR_CHANGED,
                        changeGroutColor, GroutEvent);
    addContextListener(GroutEvent.COLOR_LOADED,
                        changeGroutColor, GroutEvent);
    addContextListener(DesignEvent.DESIGN_COLORS_CHANGED,
                        redrawGrid, DesignEvent);
    dispatch(new GridReadyEvent(GridReadyEvent.READY));
}

protected function changeSelectionColor(e:TileSupplyEvent):void
{
    view.selectionColor = e.color;
}

protected function changeGroutColor(e:GroutEvent):void
{
    view.groutColor = e.color;
}

protected function redrawGrid(e:DesignEvent):void
{
    view.applyColorsToWholeGrid(e.colors);
}
}
```

In GridViewMediator.as above you can see that the view is being injected. The view is temporarily mapped in the injector by the mediatorMap, so that when your mediator is created, the view is injected against this class. Mediators also have a generic DisplayObject version of your view held in the viewComponent property. It is generally a lot more convenient to have a strongly typed version of your view to avoid casting.

Avoid logic in your Mediators

For newcomers, the mediator map is probably the most addictive and immediately attractive aspect of Robotlegs. It is also by far the most dangerous. It provides a method for connecting your view to your application without your view having any awareness of the app it sits in, and used well it's a very clean bridge between these two tiers of your application.

The danger is that, because your mediator is free to be injected with models and services too, you can abuse your mediator to create a 'quick fix' monster controller, which then rapidly develops into a tightly coupled scramble of logic that is duplicated elsewhere and is very brittle when it comes to making changes in your classes.

It is important to avoid logical code in your mediators as much as possible. They are *not* intended to make decisions for your application. They are intended to provide that bridge between the view and the rest of the application. Avoid the use of switch, for, for each, and if statements in your mediators *as much as possible*. Sometimes it can't be avoided. You have to use one of these logical blocks to do your work. It is a warning flag; stop and think about where this logic really belongs. Should it be a decision made by the view? Can we move it to a command that organizes the data before sending it to the mediator? Is this domain logic that belongs on a model that notifies the mediator?

The real key to avoiding trouble in this area is to remember that the mediator is not your view tier. Mediators sit *between* your view components and the other actors in your application. It is often tempting to reach into the view and perform complex operations—making new children to add, affecting layout, or directly manipulating properties. It is much better to define and utilize API methods on the mediated view instead of performing these actions within the mediator itself.

The mediator is a bridge. It's the glue between your view and your application, but it's not truly part of either of them. If you consistently challenge yourself, when adding code to a mediator, with the question "is this view code, app code, or glue code?" you should stay on track—only the glue code belongs here.

With those warnings in mind, here's the really fun part: the framework creates, runs, cleans up after and destroys your mediators for you. All *you* have to do is map them to your views.

Do your wiring in onRegister()

After your mediator has been created, and the view is injected into the mediator, and the mediatorMap thinks the view is ready (straight away for non-Flex views, after creationComplete for Flex-views), the MediatorMap runs a function called onRegister in your mediator.

onRegister is the function that you override in your own mediator to get your wiring set up.

```
override public function onRegister():void
{
    //we pick up user actions and translate them for the app
    addViewListener(MouseEvent.CLICK, submitUserDetails, MouseEvent);

    //we pick up app events and translate them for the view
    addContextListener(UserEvent.LOGIN_FAILED, showErrors, UserEvent);
}
```

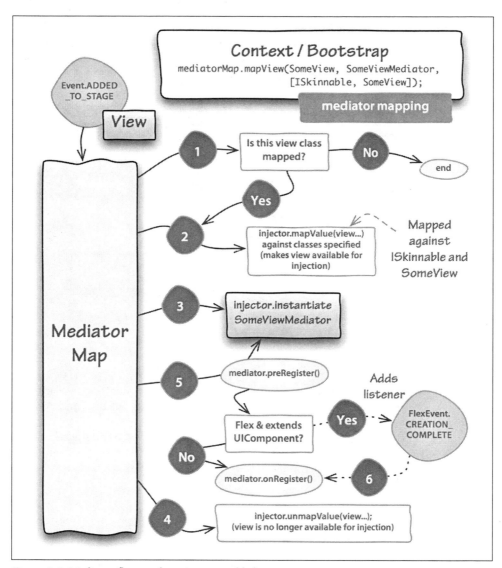

Figure 8-1. Mediator flow—when views are added

Mediator timing issues in Flex

In a Flex application, your mediators won't have access to the initialization methods of the component object lifecycle. The `MediatorMap` waits for the view to dispatch a `creationComplete` event before running the mediator's `onRegister()` method.

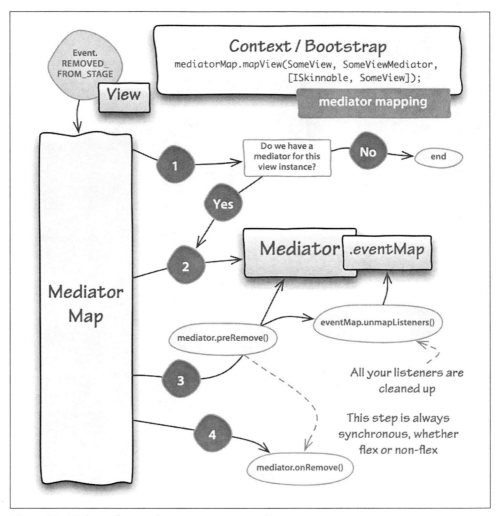

Figure 8-2. Mediator flow—when views are removed

 Note: Flash Player version 9.0.16 doesn't dispatch `Event.ADDED_TO_STAGE` or `Event.REMOVED_FROM_STAGE`. As a result, the mediator map can't hear views landing on the context view, and won't create and destroy mediators automatically.

The flash timeline can also be erratic—these events aren't consistently dispatched when views come and go in timeline animations.

These problems have workarounds. Come and talk to us on the forum and we'll help you find the best solution for your specific use case.

Mediators have a very narrow scope, essentially doing two jobs—listening for events on the view and then translating these into application events to be dispatched to the shared event dispatcher, and listening for application events on the shared event dispatcher and translating these into actions on the view API.

You should never add your event listeners to the view or the shared event dispatcher directly—instead the mediator contains an instance of the `EventMap` which takes care of listeners in a more convenient and more reliable way.

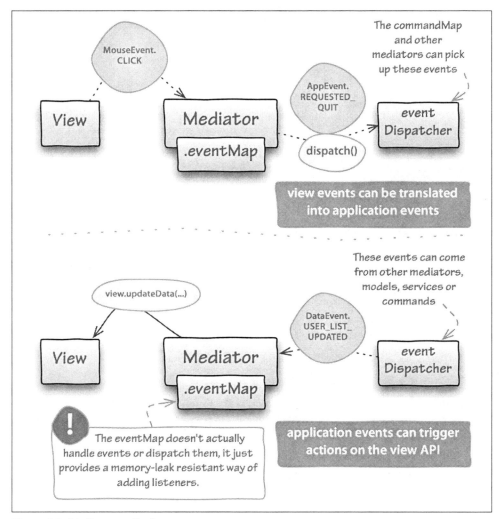

Figure 8-3. Mediator traffic flow

Using the EventMap

The main benefit of using the eventMap to wire your listeners in the mediator is that when the view leaves the stage and the mediator is destroyed, all those mappings will be automatically cleaned up, avoiding pesky memory leaks.

Mediators are equipped with two convenient methods for adding listeners to the EventMap. These methods are addViewListener() and addContextListener(). These are syntactical sugar and are functionally equivalent to using the EventMap directly. Take a look at what they are doing in the Mediator base class.

Example 8-3. Mediator.as has helper methods to make your code cleaner and easier to read

```
/**
 * Syntactical sugar for mapping a listener to the viewComponent
 */
protected function addViewListener(type:String, listener:Function,
                                   eventClass:Class = null,
                                   useCapture:Boolean = false, priority:int = 0,
                                   useWeakReference:Boolean = true):void
{
    eventMap.mapListener(IEventDispatcher(viewComponent), type, listener,
        eventClass, useCapture, priority, useWeakReference);
}

/**
 * Syntactical sugar for mapping a listener to an IEventDispatcher
 */
protected function addContextListener(type:String, listener:Function,
                                      eventClass:Class = null,
                                      useCapture:Boolean = false, priority:int = 0,
                                      useWeakReference:Boolean = true):void
    {
    eventMap.mapListener(eventDispatcher, type, listener,
        eventClass, useCapture, priority, useWeakReference);
}
```

Use the 'eventClass' parameter to make mappings that are type safe

An important criticism of the AS3 Event system is that it relies on 'magic' strings and isn't type safe. If your application contains two events with the same string-constants, you can experience bugs where handlers run unexpectedly, because an event with the same string has been fired.

In a non-framework based application you'll usually be listening directly to individual objects for their events, so the opportunity for cross-firings is quite small. The Robotlegs shared event dispatcher has the benefit of decoupling the listening-relationship from the source of the event—I don't care who fired ApplicationEvent.QUIT, I just want to know that it fired—but the flip side is a much increased likelihood of event-name overlap bugs.

One solution is to include the event class name, or even the whole package, in the event string. But this still ultimately relies on the assumption that every event string is unique. The event map offers an eventClass argument in the methods for adding listeners. This solves the problem by binding your listeners to the event class as well as the type string.

If you don't provide the optional eventClass parameter when you make the mapping, your mapping will be made against the base Event type, meaning that any event with the correct String for its type property will trigger your handler to run.

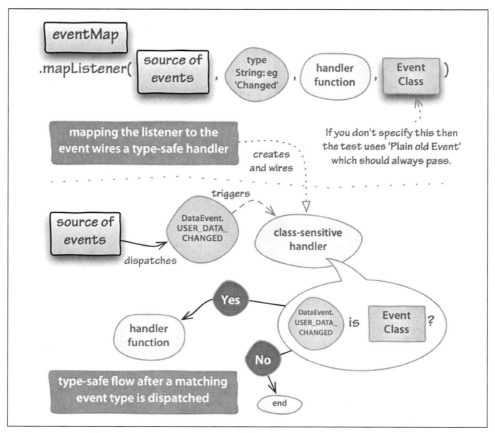

Figure 8-4. How the EventMap processes type-safe mappings

You can do manual clean-up in onRemove

If all you've done in your onRegister function is use the event map to map listeners, you won't need to do anything extra in your mediator to clean it up when it is destroyed —triggered by the view being removed from the stage. But if there's something that you need to clean up manually to avoid memory leaks then overriding the onRemove method is the way to do it.

Why can't Mediators be injected into other objects?

In Robotlegs 1.6 we've fully removed mediator mappings on the injector, so it shouldn't be possible to inject a mediator into another class unless you were to set up the injection manually (if you want to do this then come talk to us about it on the forum, there are ways but they're usually not the best solution available.) But in earlier versions of Robotlegs it was possible to inject mediators as a side-effect of how the mediator map did its job.

The number one reason not to inject mediators is that your mediator will then persist even after the view has left the stage, and wham!—suddenly you've got memory leaks and unexpected behaviors all over the place.

But from a more theoretical approach, mediators should have no API beyond the functions they override (usually just `onRegister` and maybe `onRemove`). In their role as 'glue code' they shouldn't be available for other objects to act upon, and anyway—what would those other objects be asking them to do?

Usually, when people start asking about injecting mediators, they're worried about proliferation of custom events, and are looking to avoid this by communicating directly between the mediators of several different views. Events are cheap, easy to create (if you disagree with this then we think you need a new IDE!) and they keep your code decoupled. Embrace the many-small-classes approach and you'll see the pay offs. Just remember to name your events descriptively—most 'I don't like loads of small classes, it's confusing and I don't know where to look for code' issues are really about problems with class and event naming.

Table 8-1.

Good Event names	Bad Event names
DesignCreationEvent.DESIGN_CREATED	CreationEvent.CREATED
UserModelEvent.USER_SAVED	ModelEvent.SAVED
StatsServiceEvent.SUBMISSION_COMPLETED	ServiceEvent.SUCCESS

Working with complex composite views

You always have access to the `eventMap` property itself, so if you wanted to listen to two child buttons on your view, that were exposed through getters, you can use the event map to manage this:

Example 8-4. MosiacTool: TileSupplyDetailViewMediator.as maps listeners to two Button subcomponents of the mediated view

```
override public function onRegister():void
{
    eventMap.mapListener(view.deleteButton, MouseEvent.CLICK,
                                    dispatchDeletionRequest, MouseEvent);
```

```
        eventMap.mapListener(view.radioButton, MouseEvent.CLICK,
                                dispatchSupplySelected, MouseEvent);
        addViewListener(ColorChangeEvent.CHANGED,
                                dispatchColorChange, ColorChangeEvent);
        addContextListener(TileSupplyEvent.QUANTITY_CHANGED,
                                updateCount, TileSupplyEvent);
}
```

There are more elegant solutions that avoid you having to expose those child buttons
to the mediator—because of course exposing them means that any object with access
to the view is free to move these buttons, change their alpha, make them invisible—
yikes! One option is to use custom events on your views—these could belong to the
view, rather than being application events, so that your view can be reused in a totally
different application.

*Example 8-5. KanbanApp: TaskLane.mxml listens for a deleteTask Event from an ItemRenderer and
dispatches the DeleteTaskEvent*

```
private function deleteTaskHandler(event:Event):void
{
    dispatchEvent(new DeleteTaskEvent(taskList.selectedItem as Task));
}
```

> An alternative approach to managing complex views is to use the
> AS3Signals library, a powerful twist on the AS3 event system, originated
> by Robert Penner and already very popular. For more details on that
> approach, check out the Power Ups section: "Use Signals between com-
> plex views and their mediators" on page 106.

Using the same mediator with more than one view

Sometimes you'll have two views that can be mediated in the same way. Perhaps one
of the views extends the other. A common example is the case of a nested menu where
sections and subsections might have a different appearance and internal behavior, but
behave the same in terms of how they relate to the application. Where the user is rolling
over or clicking a section or subsection, you want the mediator to send an event in-
forming the application that something has been rolled over or selected, so you want
to map both view types against a single mediator type.

The catch is that your mediator expects a view to be injected against an exact type. If
the mediator expects SectionButton to be injected, when the mediator for
SubSectionButton is created, it will complain about a 'null injection error'. This is because the mediatorMap automatically injects the view against its
Fully Qualified Class Name, and doesn't automatically inject against all its superTypes
and interfaces. The work around is to specify extra classes that you would like the view
to be mapped against:

Example 8-6. To reuse a mediator against a subtype or interface, you need to specify the classes to inject against when you make the mapping

```
mediatorMap.mapView(SectionButton, SectionButtonMediator);
// this will ensure the SubSectionButton is mapped against
// the SectionButton class that the mediator expects
// this 3rd parameter - 'injectViewAs' - can be a Class or an array of Classes
mediatorMap.mapView(SubSectionButton, SectionButtonMediator, SectionButton);
```

Another common workflow is to extend a base mediator for sub-typed views—perhaps your SubSectionButton needs some extra behavior, and so you want to extend SectionButtonMediator to create SubSectionButtonMediator and add the extra behavior. In the case where you're using the extra API that is unique to SubSectionButton, you'll need to inject the view as both the SectionButton—to fulfil the injection in the base SectionButtonMediator, and the SubSectionButton, for the SubSectionButtonMediator to use:

Example 8-7. To use a mediator which subclasses another mediator, you need to specify the classes to inject against when you make the mapping

```
mediatorMap.mapView(SectionButton, SectionButtonMediator);
// this will ensure the SubSectionButton is mapped against
// the SectionButton class that the superclass mediator expects
// and against the SubSectionButton class that the subclass mediator expects
mediatorMap.mapView(SubSectionButton, SubSectionButtonMediator,
                                    [SectionButton, SubSectionButton]);
```

♪♪ The Robotlegs Way

Keep mediators light and logic free

Flash applications are view-centric. We are primarily front end developers. This means that your views are the focus of your application, especially for your clients and their customers interact with them. Mediators are very close to your view components and can be a very attractive place to insert all sorts of functionality.

Using mediators to do small pieces of work is convenient, but solutions born out of convenience often lead to trouble down the road. In the real world we've seen mediators grow to gigantic proportions. Mediators that hold state and contain endless logic. Mediators that dig into view components and manipulate properties and orchestrate complex manipulations of the state of a view. 1,200 lines of madness that ultimately become a constant source of defects.

We want to convince you that it doesn't have to be this way. By keeping a few principles in your mind as you build your mediators, you should be able to avoid this. When you stumble across a monster mediator that's dragging the codebase down, you can apply these same principles in refactoring the offending bits out. ♪♪

A good Mediator is just a mailman

A mediator should never hold state. It is not the place to add flags or attempt to manage individual objects for future access. This is a job for your models. Mediators are temporary. They are destroyed and freshly created as the view comes and goes from the stage.

You can inject your mediator with any object that you've mapped on the Robotlegs Injector. This means that it's possible to inject models and services into your mediators and work on them directly.

However, doing this couples your mediator to the model or service and is potentially dangerous. If you are injecting models and services, you should at least be injecting them against interfaces and not concrete classes. Better, the interface should be a sub-interface that only exposes methods that are safe to use—perhaps a read-only interface for a model. Injecting models and services into mediators should be done with care; continuously challenge yourself about whether you've overstepped the level of coupling that is appropriate.

Your mediator is inherently lazy. It should perform the minimum work possible to get its job done. If it needs to do complex translations on values between the application events and the view events or API, consider using a helper class to encapsulate this logic. Sometimes you need to go a step further, and break the process up, allowing a Command to catch the original event, use a model or helper to parse it to the form the view needs, and dispatch it ready-baked for the mediator to catch and pass on.

Signs that your mediator is over-involved:

- Implementing view logic or view control such as animation or input validation
- Reaching into the view and manipulating properties and child views directly rather than using the view's API
- Properties holding state on behalf of the view
- Switch statements checking view properties before deciding what API to run
- Switch statements checking view properties before deciding which event to dispatch
- Injecting another object in order to use its properties in a conditional
- Complex conditional switches on event properties (checking an ID to see if this message applies to your view is as far as it should extend)
- Injecting more than one view
- Injecting another mediator

Keeping your mediator lazy enough

Bring to mind the laziest person you've ever met. Perhaps it was your kid brother or sister—13 seems to be a peak age for laziness. Perhaps it was an ex-colleague. Perhaps it was some kid in your class at school. Anyway—imagine that person's response when they were asked to do a job. Probably it was something like "Do I *have* to?" or "Can't someone else do it?"—maybe they even made excuses "But (your name) is sooo much better at mowing the lawn than I am!" When you're programming your Mediators, bring this person to mind. Allow your Mediator to channel that reluctance and you won't go far wrong.

Signs that you need another mediator

As you add functionality to your view components, their associated mediators will grow. They will listen for more events from the view. They will listen for more events from the application context. As your mediator gains weight, you can break it down into smaller mediators governing individual components.

How do you know when it is time to separate a sub-component and provide it with its own mediator? There is no fixed answer for this. It depends on the view component and the application. If a mediator is listening to more than six events, start to really think about it. If it is listening for more than 12 then it can probably be broken down into smaller pieces.

If you are struggling with mediator granularity—finding it hard to decide whether a sub-component warrants its own mediator—try reversing the decision process. Assume *every* view or sub-component deserves its own mediator and then eliminate those which don't require direct wiring to the application, and group only those that really belong together. It's sometimes perfectly valid to give an individual button its own mediator.

Never put view logic into the mediator.

Never, ever, put view logic into the mediator. Only translation—or 'glue'—logic. View logic includes input validation and animation of the view and its child views. If you need view logic that is separated from the view itself, you should use a three-layer approach.

Your mediator may then sometimes respond to events on the shared event dispatcher by using the API of the view controller rather than using the view API directly. It all depends on the purpose of this view controller.

But how do you get the view controller involved with the view? Ideally you want this to happen when you instantiate the view, but if the parent doing the instantiation has no business knowing about the view controller, what then? You could, in this situation,

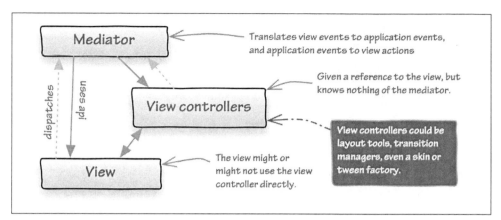

Figure 8-5. Use a three-layer approach to avoid putting logic in mediators

inject a view-controller factory into your mediator—and exploit the fact that the factory is persistent even though the mediator isn't. Leave the factory to decide whether this view needs to be processed or whether it has already been handled.

Alternatively, you could inject the correct view-controller directly, most appropriate if there's only one and it's not too stateful, for example a transition manager. There are numerous approaches, each with benefits and potential problems. The important thing is that you really consider your choice—don't just reach for the [Inject] tag every time.

CHAPTER 9

Working with Robotlegs: Rich Examples

The applications we've built as examples are too large to describe fully in this book. Rather than build a shallow demo small enough to fill that role, we decided to pull out specific features from the example applications, running through the configuration, models, services, views, mediators and commands that come together to implement each feature.

To illustrate the balance of flexibility and consistency that Robotlegs can help you achieve, we've selected user stories common to many Flash and Flex applications:

- Keeping the model aligned with user actions on a rich interface
- Creating a new 'something'

Feature implementation walk-through: Mosaic Tool

The Mosaic Tool is an example of an application where the model exists to represent the view, and not the other way around. In a twitter app, for example, the view exists to allow you to read and write the 'messages' which are the primary concern. Although most of the principles are common to both kinds of applications, a genuinely view-driven app creates a couple of specific challenges for the developer.

Challenge 1: Keeping things on a need-to-know basis

In our model, tile supplies are represented by VOs with three properties:

- ID (a uint unique to each supply)
- color
- quantity

It's necessary for each supply to have a unique ID because it's valid for the user to set two supplies to the same color—particularly if they're experimenting with how a pattern looks with different combinations of colored tiles.

So, from the model's point of view, tile supplies are identified by ID. The design model is a grid (a vector of vectors of uints) capturing the ID of the tile supply assigned to each square. If you were to dump the design model to text it would look something like:

```
0, 1, 3, 1, 0, 1, 3, 1, 0
0, 3, 2, 3, 0, 3, 2, 3, 0
0, 1, 3, 1, 5, 1, 3, 1, 0
0, 3, 2, 3, 4, 3, 2, 3, 0
0, 1, 3, 1, 5, 1, 3, 1, 0
0, 3, 2, 3, 0, 3, 2, 3, 0
0, 1, 3, 1, 0, 1, 3, 1, 0
```

So, the model is mostly concerned with IDs, with the exception of the individual TileSupplyVOs themselves, which know their color. In contrast, the view is only concerned with colors. The user is not interested in the IDs of the tile supplies they are working with, only with what color each supply is and what color each tile is.

To avoid bothering our models and views with details they're not interested in, the Mosaic Tool was architected using the following rules:

- The model will only know about tile supply IDs
- The view will only know about tile colors
- The only exceptions will be those directly involved in representing the tile supplies:
  - The TileSupplyVOs will contain their ID and their color
  - The TileSupplyDetailViews will hold a reference to the ID of the supply they represent, so that we can know which view corresponds to which model when the view or model changes

Challenge 2: Keeping the view snappy

A criticism of the mediators-and-commands approach to building rich applications is that the cycle between user action and the view updating can be slow. For user actions done occasionally this isn't important, but when the user clicks the tiles on their mosaic design, we want the color change to be as fast as possible.

For this reason, the GridView itself always knows what the current tile supply color is. This way it can respond to tile clicks by immediately updating the color of the specified tile, before the updates to the models are carried out. In some scenarios, allowing the view to update itself without the model validating the change would be dangerous. In this use case the only possible outcome of a tile being clicked is that it changes to the selected color, so we don't need to involve the model in validating the user action before we update the view.

Keeping the models in line with the visual design

When the user clicks a tile on the grid, the following things need to happen:

- The tile needs to change to the current selected supply color
- The selected tile supply needs to increment its count
- The tile supply that the tile used to be needs to decrement its count
- The tile supply views need to show the updated counts
- The model needs to record the change to the design

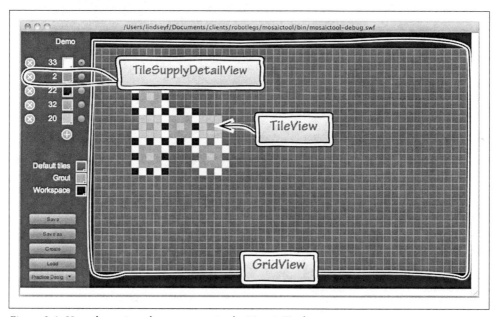

Figure 9-1. How these view classes appear in the Mosaic Tool

In Robotlegs, these steps come together via the shared event dispatcher. Mediators listen and dispatch on it for their views. Commands triggered by events on it do work on models and services. The model and services dispatch update events and the mediators pass relevant information to their views.

When the user clicks a tile, the Mosaic Tool enters into a sequence of eleven steps:

❶ The TileView dispatches MouseEvent.CLICK

❷ GridTilesView (a Sprite holding only the tiles) checks the row and column of this particular tile, and runs a callback that it was passed when it was created by its parent, the GridView

❸ The GridView immediately runs the color setter on the TileView that was originally clicked (it has been passed in the callback)

❹ GridView dispatches a `TileColorChangeEvent.CHANGED` event, carrying the row and column (it also carries the selected color but in this situation it's unimportant)

❺ The `GridViewMediator` redispatches this event to the whole application

❻ Because this event has been mapped to the `UpdateDesignCommand`, the command is created, and injected with the `DesignModel`, the `TileSuppliesModel` (which manages all the different tile supplies), and also the event that triggered it

❼ The `UpdateDesignCommand` is executed. It gets the current selected ID from the `TileSuppliesModel`, then asks the `DesignModel` to change the tile colour at that row and column (from the event) to the current selected ID. The `DesignModel` returns the ID that this entry in the grid previously held (this is the supply we need to decrement the count on)

❽ The command tells the `TileSuppliesModel` that the tiles have been switched

❾ The `TileSuppliesModel` updates the counts on the relevant `TileSupplyVOs` and dispatches two `TileSupplyEvent.QUANTITY_CHANGED` events with the VOs properties as payload

❿ All of the `TileSupplyDetailViewMediators` pick up these events and handle them...

⓫ ... If the ID on the event matches the ID of the view they are managing, the handler updates the count on the `TileSupplyDetailView`

The crucial Robotlegs mappings that tie it all together

We need to configure Robotlegs to know how to mediate our views, which commands to run in response to different events, and which classes to use to fulfil our injected models and services:

```
//in BoostrapViewMediators.as
mediatorMap.mapView(TileSupplyDetailView, TileSupplyDetailViewMediator);

// in BoostrapTileSupplyCommands.as
commandMap.mapEvent(TileColorChangeEvent.CHANGED,
                            UpdateDesignCommand, TileColorChangeEvent);

// in BootstrapModels.as
injector.mapSingletonOf(IMosaicDesignModel, MosaicDesignModel);
injector.mapSingletonOf(ITileSuppliesModel, TileSuppliesModel);
```

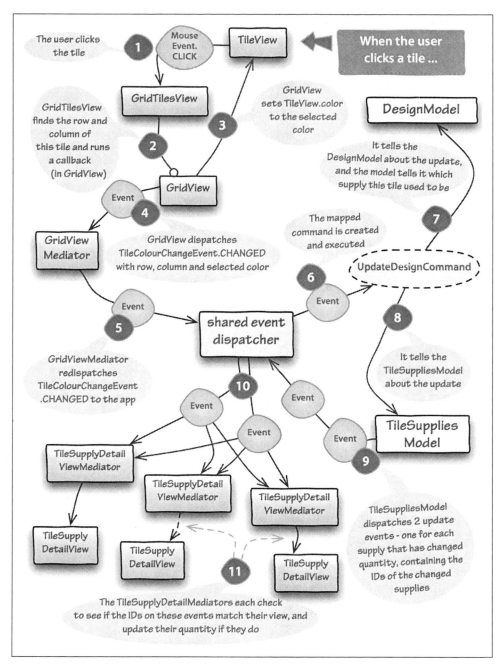

The user clicks the tile

1 Mouse Event. CLICK → TileView

When the user clicks a tile ...

GridTilesView finds the row and column of this tile and runs a callback (in GridView)

GridTilesView

2

3

GridView sets TileView.color to the selected color

DesignModel

It tells the DesignModel about the update, and the model tells it which supply this tile used to be

GridView

7

Event **4**

The mapped command is created and executed

GridView Mediator

GridView dispatches TileColourChangeEvent.CHANGED with row, column and selected color

6 Event

UpdateDesignCommand

Event **5**

shared event dispatcher

8

GridViewMediator redispatches TileColourChangeEvent .CHANGED to the app

10

Event

Event

It tells the TileSuppliesModel about the update

Event

TileSupplies Model

Event

Event **9**

TileSupplyDetail ViewMediator

TileSupplyDetail ViewMediator

TileSupplyDetail ViewMediator

TileSupply DetailView

TileSupply DetailView

11

TileSupply DetailView

TileSuppliesModel dispatches 2 update events - one for each supply that has changed quantity, containing the IDs of the changed supplies

The TileSupplyDetailMediators each check to see if the IDs on these events match their view, and update their quantity if they do

Figure 9-2. When the user clicks a tile, the Mosaic Tool enters into a sequence of 11 steps

The tile color update again, but this time with code

The numbers on the code samples match with the step numbers given in the preceding list.

Example 9-1. When the user clicks a tile...

```
package mosaic.view.grid
{
  public class GridTilesView extends Sprite
  {
      protected var _tileFactory:ITileFactory;
      protected var _tiles:Vector.<Vector.<ITileView>>;
      protected var _positionsByTiles:Dictionary;
      protected var _clickHandler:Function;

      public function GridTilesView(tileFactory:ITileFactory, rows:uint, columns:uint,
                                    clickHandler:Function)
      {
          _tileFactory = tileFactory;
          _positionsByTiles = new Dictionary();
          _clickHandler = clickHandler;
          addTiles(rows, columns);
      }
      ...

      protected function generateTile(i:uint, j:uint):ITileView
      {
          var nextTile:ITileView = _tileFactory.createTile();
          _positionsByTiles[nextTile] = new Point(j, i);
          nextTile.addEventListener(MouseEvent.CLICK, handleTileClick, false, 0, true);❶
          addTileAtPosition(nextTile, i, j);
          return nextTile;
      }
      ...

      protected function handleTileClick(e:MouseEvent):void
      {
          var selectedTile:ITileView = (e.target as ITileView);
          var column:uint = _positionsByTiles[selectedTile].x;
          var row:uint = _positionsByTiles[selectedTile].y;

          _clickHandler(selectedTile, row, column);❷
      }
  }
}


package mosaic.view.grid
{
  public class GridView extends Sprite implements IGridView
  {
      protected var _selectionColor:uint;
      protected var _groutColor:uint;
      protected var _tileFactory:ITileFactory;
```

```
        protected var _groutLines:GroutLinesView;
        protected var _tilesView:GridTilesView;

        public function GridView(tileFactory:ITileFactory)
        {
            _tileFactory = tileFactory;
            _selectionColor = new ContrastingColor(tileFactory.defaultColor).color;
        }
        ...

        protected function changeTileColor(selectedTile:ITileView,
                                            row:uint, column:uint):void
        {
            selectedTile.color = _selectionColor;❸
            dispatchEvent(new TileColorChangeEvent(TileColorChangeEvent.CHANGED,
                                        row, column, _selectionColor));❹
        }
        ...
    }
}


package mosaic.view.grid
{
  public class GridViewMediator extends Mediator
  {
      [Inject]
      public var view:GridView;

      override public function onRegister():void
      {
          addViewListener(TileColorChangeEvent.CHANGED, dispatch, TileColorChangeEvent);❺
          addContextListener(TileSupplyEvent.SUPPLY_SELECTED,
                                            changeSelectionColor, TileSupplyEvent);
          addContextListener(TileSupplyEvent.SELECTED_SUPPLY_COLOR_CHANGED,
                                            changeSelectionColor, TileSupplyEvent);
          addContextListener(GroutEvent.COLOR_CHANGED, changeGroutColor, GroutEvent);
          addContextListener(GroutEvent.COLOR_LOADED, changeGroutColor, GroutEvent);
          addContextListener(DesignEvent.DESIGN_COLORS_CHANGED, redrawGrid, DesignEvent);
          dispatch(new GridReadyEvent(GridReadyEvent.READY));
      }
      ...
  }
}


package mosaic.controller.commands
{
  public class UpdateDesignCommand extends Command
  {
      [Inject]
      public var designModel:IMosaicDesignModel;

      [Inject]
      public var tileSuppliesModel:ITileSuppliesModel;
```

```
        [Inject]
        public var tileColorChangeEvent:TileColorChangeEvent;

        override public function execute():void ❻
        {
            var row:uint = tileColorChangeEvent.row;
            var column:uint = tileColorChangeEvent.column;

            var idNow:uint = tileSuppliesModel.selectedSupplyID;

            var idWas:uint = designModel.changeTileColorAt(row, column, idNow); ❼

            if (idNow != idWas)
            {
                tileSuppliesModel.switchTiles(idWas, idNow); ❽
            }
        }
    }
}


package mosaic.model
{
  public class MosaicDesignModel extends Actor implements IMosaicDesignModel
  {
      protected var _designGrid:Vector.<Vector.<uint>>;

      ...

      public function changeTileColorAt(row:uint, column:uint, colorID:uint):uint
      {
          var colorIDWas:uint = _designGrid[row][column];
          _designGrid[row][column] = colorID;
          return colorIDWas;
      }
  }
}


package mosaic.model
{
  public class TileSuppliesModel extends Actor implements ITileSuppliesModel
  {
      protected var _supplyList:TileSuppliesList;

      public function switchTiles(idWas:uint, idNow:uint):void
      {
          supplyWithID(idWas).count -= 1;
          supplyWithID(idNow).count += 1;
          dispatchTileSupplyEvent(TileSupplyEvent.QUANTITY_CHANGED, supplyWithID(idWas));❾
          dispatchTileSupplyEvent(TileSupplyEvent.QUANTITY_CHANGED, supplyWithID(idNow));
      }
      ...
```

```
    protected function supplyWithID(id:uint):TileSupplyVO
    {
        return _supplyList.supplyWithID(id) || new NullTileSupplyVO();
    }

    protected function dispatchTileSupplyEvent(type:String, vo:TileSupplyVO):void
    {
        dispatch(new TileSupplyEvent(type, vo.id, vo.color, vo.count));
    }
  }
}


package mosaic.view.tilesupply
{
  public class TileSupplyDetailViewMediator extends Mediator
  {
    [Inject]
    public var view:TileSupplyDetailView;

    override public function onRegister():void
    {
        eventMap.mapListener(view.deleteButton, MouseEvent.CLICK,
                                        dispatchDeletionRequest, MouseEvent);
        eventMap.mapListener(view.radioButton, MouseEvent.CLICK,
                                        dispatchSupplySelected, MouseEvent);
        addViewListener(ColorChangeEvent.CHANGED,
                                        dispatchColorChange, ColorChangeEvent);
        addContextListener(TileSupplyEvent.QUANTITY_CHANGED,
                                        updateCount, TileSupplyEvent); ❿
    }
    ...

    protected function updateCount(e:TileSupplyEvent):void
    {
        if (e.id == view.id) ⓫
        {
            view.count = e.count;
        }
    }
  }
}
```

Feature implementation walk-through: Personal Kanban App

The Personal Kanban App is an 'always up to date' application. Instead of having to manually save changes, the current status of the user's tasks is tracked in an SQL database as they add and adjust tasks.

Where the Mosaic Tool allows the view to drive the model, the Person Kanban has to defer all decisions to the models and services. If the view shows a status which hasn't been successfully created in the database then the next time the user comes to use the application it will appear to have 'lost' their data.

It's also possible for the status lists to 'refuse' entry to a task, perhaps setting a limit on how many tasks can be in the 'doing' list. This is very much an application in which the view is a slave to the models and services.

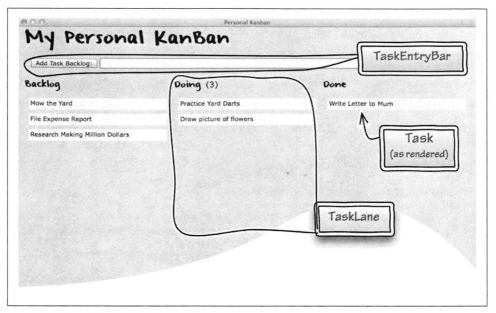

Figure 9-3. How the Kanban classes relate to the view

How new tasks are entered

When the user adds a new task, the following things need to happen:

- A task with this name has to be created in the database
- The task list needs to be updated to contain this task
- A task having the name has to be displayed in the backlog list (only if the previous steps are successful)

When the user submits a new task, the Personal Kanban app enters into a sequence of thirteen steps:

1. The TaskEntryBar addTask button responds to the user's click (❸)
2. The TaskEntryBar addTask button responds to the user's click (❶)
3. The TaskEntryBar dispatches a SaveTaskEvent* with this Task as payload (❷)

---

* Joel uses a one-type per event strategy so type constants on events are only needed when listening, not when dispatching

4. This event triggers the SaveTaskCommand to be created and injected with the event and also an ITaskService (❹)

5. The SaveTaskCommand is executed, and asks the TaskService to save the task (❺)

6. The TaskService asks the SQLRunnerDelegate to put the task into the database, giving it handlers to run on success and failure (❽)

7. The entry success handler receives the newly created ID for that task (IDs are created by the database) then asks the SQLRunnerDelegate to load that particular task (by id), again passing handlers for success and failure (❾)

8. The load success handler takes the task that was loaded and asks the task list model to update this task (❻)

9. The handler also asks the StatusListModel to add this task to its status (❼)

10. The StatusListModel checks whether this status (lane) has any space left, and if it does then it adds the task to its new status (❿)

11. If the task already had a status, the task is removed from its old status (⓫)

12. The Status VOs are bindable, so when updated, they dispatch their binding change events (⓬)

13. The TaskLanes receive the updates from the StatusVOs to which they are bound, and the newly created task is displayed in the user's 'backlog' lane (⓭)

The crucial Robotlegs mappings that make this sequence work

We need to configure Robotlegs to know how to mediate our views, which commands to run in response to different events, and which classes to use to fulfil our injected models and services:

```
//in PersonalKanbanContext.as
mediatorMap.mapView(TaskLane, TaskLaneMediator);
mediatorMap.mapView(TaskEntryBar, TaskEntryBarMediator);

injector.mapSingletonOf(ITaskService, SQLTaskService);

injector.mapSingleton(StatusListModel);
injector.mapSingleton(TaskListModel);

commandMap.mapEvent(SaveTaskEvent.SAVE, SaveTaskCommand);
```

Adding a new task again, but this time with code

The numbers on the code samples match with the numbers given at the end of each step in the preceding list.

```
TaskEntryBar.mxml:

<s:HGroup...>

    <fx:Script><![CDATA[
```

```
            private function taskInput_enterHandler():void
            {
                var task:Task = new Task(taskInput.text); ❶

                dispatchEvent(new SaveTaskEvent(task)); ❷

                reset();
            }

            public function reset():void
            {
                taskInput.text = "";
            }
            ]]></fx:Script>

    <s:Button id="addTask"
              label="Add Task Backlog:"
              click="taskInput_enterHandler()"/> ❸
    <s:TextInput id="taskInput"
                 width="100%"
                 enter="taskInput_enterHandler()"/>
</s:HGroup>


package robotlegs.examples.kanban.controller
{
    public class SaveTaskCommand ❹
    {
        [Inject]
        public var event:SaveTaskEvent;

        [Inject]
        public var taskService:ITaskService;

        public function execute():void
        {
            taskService.save(event.task); ❺
        }
    }
}


package robotlegs.examples.kanban.service
{
    public class SQLTaskService extends Actor implements ITaskService
    {
        [Inject]
        public var sqlRunner:ISQLRunnerDelegate;

        [Inject]
        public var statusListModel:StatusListModel;

        [Inject]
        public var taskListModel:TaskListModel;
```

```
...
public function loadTaskById(id:int):void
{
    sqlRunner.execute(LOAD_TASK_SQL, {taskId:id}, loadTaskResultHandler, Task);
}

private function loadTaskResultHandler(result:SQLResult):void
{
    var task:Task = result.data[0] as Task;
    var taskStatus:Status = statusListModel.getStatusFromId(task.statusId);

    task = taskListModel.updateTask(task); ❻

    statusListModel.addTaskToStatus(task, taskStatus); ❼
}

public function save(task:Task):void
{
    var params:Object = task.toParamObject();

    sqlRunner.executeModify(Vector.<QueuedStatement>(
            [new QueuedStatement(SAVE_TASK_SQL, params)]),
                        saveTaskResultHandler, databaseErrorHandler); ❽
}

private function saveTaskResultHandler(results:Vector.<SQLResult>):void ❾
{
    var result:SQLResult = results[0];
    if (result.rowsAffected > 0)
    {
        var id:Number = result.lastInsertRowID;
        loadTaskById(id);
    }
}

public function deleteTask(task:Task):void
{
    sqlRunner.executeModify(Vector.<QueuedStatement>(
                [new QueuedStatement(DELETE_TASK_SQL,{taskId:task.taskId})]),
                                deleteTaskResult, databaseErrorHandler);
}

private function deleteTaskResult(results:Vector.<SQLResult>):void
{
    //pass
}

private function databaseErrorHandler(error:SQLError):void
{
    dispatch(new DatabaseErrorHandlerEvent(error.message));
}
...
}
```

```
    }

package robotlegs.examples.kanban.model
{
    public class StatusListModel extends Actor
    {
        private var _statuses:ArrayCollection;

        ...

        public function addTaskToStatus(task:Task, status:Status):void
        {
            if(status.isOverLimit)
            {
                dispatch(new StatusTaskLimitReachedEvent());
                return;
            }

            if (!status.tasks.contains(task))
            {
                status.tasks.addItem(task); ❿
                if (task.status)
                    removeTaskFromStatus(task, task.status); ⓫
                task.status = status;
            }
        }

        private function removeTaskFromStatus(task:Task, status:Status):void
        {
            if (status.tasks.contains(task))
                status.tasks.removeItemAt(status.tasks.getItemIndex(task));
        }
        ...
    }
}


package robotlegs.examples.kanban.model.vo
{
    [Bindable] ⓬
    public class Status
    {
        public function Status(label:String = "")
        {
            this.label = label;
        }

        public var statusId:int;
        public var label:String;
        public var taskLimit:int;

        private var _tasks:ArrayCollection;

        public function get tasks():ArrayCollection
        {
```

```
            return _tasks ||= new ArrayCollection();
        }

        public function set tasks(value:ArrayCollection):void
        {
            _tasks = value;
        }
        ...
    }
}
```

TaskLane.mxml:

```
<s:ItemRenderer ...>

    ...

    <controls:TaskList
            id="taskList"
            dragEnabled="true"
            dropEnabled="true"
            dataProvider="{data.tasks}" ⓭
            dragDrop="dragDropHandler(event)"
            dragEnter="dragEnterHandler(event)"
            ...
```

How does the TaskLane.mxml know which status to bind with?

The TaskLanes are contained within a StatusGroup, which has its own StatusGroupMediator. When the status list loads, the mediator for the status group passes it the list of statuses, and each TaskLane receives a Status to bind with.

In Flex-speak: the TaskLanes are item renderers for the list of Statuses passed to the StatusGroup by it's mediator.

```
public class StatusGroupMediator extends Mediator
{
    [Inject]
    public var view:StatusGroup;

    override public function onRegister():void
    {
        addContextListener(StatusesUpdatedEvent.UPDATED, statusesLoadedHandler);
    }

    private function statusesLoadedHandler(event:StatusesUpdatedEvent):void
    {
        view.dataProvider = event.statuses;
    }
}
```

Wait, I want more examples!

We could fill hundreds more pages with examples, but if you download the source code you'll have the full source for both demos, complete with code coloring and your favourite keyboard shortcuts. We suggest that you try following through some of the Mosaic Tool and Personal Kanban user stories for yourself, and then experiment with adding and changing features. If you mess up, you can always re-download the code samples, so get stuck in!

https://examples.oreilly.com/9781449308902-files

You'll find that the demo examples also come with plenty of tests. If you've yet to integrate testing into your development process, perhaps tweaking our tests will be a good way to build your confidence. (After checking out chapter 10, which is all about testing of course!)

Here are the user stories we'd recommend you investigate:

In the Mosaic Tool:

- Updating the design when the user changes the color of a tile supply
- Creating a new design
- Save as—creating a copy of the design with a new name

In the Personal Kanban App:

- How dragging a task updates its status
- How the database is set up for the user's 'first run' of the application

Having trouble getting our code to compile?

We've tried to supply a few alternative ways of building the projects, but if we haven't come up with one that works for you, let us know what you need and we'll add it to the selection.

CHAPTER 10

Testing your Robotlegs application

We test the framework—so you don't have to

The Robotlegs creators are test nuts. This means that the core framework—the `Injector`, `EventMap`, `CommandMap`, `MediatorMap` and all the MVCS classes that you extend are well covered with tests, so you don't need to test their functionality in your own tests.

Of course, the tests aren't perfect—from time to time someone reports a strange behavior they've encountered and we realize that their particular corner-case isn't covered by the tests. So we add more tests, fix the strangeness, ensure all the existing tests still pass and then push the update.

One of the main motivators for the creation of Robotlegs was to allow us to build our own applications using TDD (Test Driven Development). In contrast to some other frameworks, choosing Robotlegs makes it easier for you to implement unit, integration and end-to-end tests. When it comes to testing your own code, you should find that it's simply a case of implementing some setup.

Your test provides the injections

Including the event dispatcher
If you're testing a class that is normally instantiated with the injector, you need your test setup to do the work the injector would do.

If your class under test extends `Actor`, `Mediator` or `Command` then the minimum you'll need to provide in the test setup is the `eventDispatcher`.

Example 10-1. MosaicTool: ConfigModelTest.as provides the eventDispatcher to the model in the setup function (AsUnit 3 tests)

```
override protected function setUp():void
{
    super.setUp();
    instance = new ConfigModel();
```

```
    instance.eventDispatcher = new EventDispatcher();
}
```

 If you are extending Actor and it seems that you could get away without providing the eventDispatcher because your code doesn't dispatch any events, you don't need to extend Actor at all!

Any other injection can be provided in whatever way suits you best—whether it's a concrete instance of the class that is injected or a stub or mock, also known as a 'test double'. In the example our test doubles are created using Mockolate's nice() function. Mockolate's nice(ISomething) creates an instance capable of standing in for the class or interface you pass to it. It's called 'nice' because it's more flexible than its counterpart, 'strict'!

Example 10-2. MosaicTool: DesignFromSolParserTest.as provides the dependencies using a mix of mocks and support objects (AsUnit 3 tests)

```
override protected function setUp():void
{
    super.setUp();
    instance = new DesignFromSolParser();
    instance.designModel = new MosaicDesignModelSupport();
    instance.designSpec = nice(IMosaicSpecModel);
    instance.tileSuppliesModel = new TileSuppliesModelSupport();

    var tileSupplyParser:TileSupplyFromSolParser = new TileSupplyFromSolParser();
    tileSupplyParser.tileAutoIncrementor = nice(IAutoIncrementor);
    instance.tileSupplyParser = tileSupplyParser;
}
```

Testing models

API methods should return values or dispatch update events on the shared event dispatcher, or both
In most circumstances, there are only three actions you can perform on a model:

- You can update it (by setting a value)
- You can manipulate it (using some kind of transformation function)
- You can ask for data from it directly (using a get or create function)

In response, the model can either return something directly there and then, or dispatch some kind of update event through its shared event dispatcher.

Your test will need to provide the eventDispatcher if it's needed, and otherwise it's a straightforward unit test.

Example 10-3. MosaicTool: TileSuppliesModelTest.as (AsUnit 3 tests)

```
public class TileSuppliesModelTest extends TestCase
{
protected var instance:TileSuppliesModel;
protected var _receivedEventsByID:Dictionary;

protected static const ADDED_ID:uint = 99;
protected static const ADDED_COLOR:uint = 0x336699;
protected static const REMOVED_ID:uint = 2;
protected static const TILES_PER_INDEX:Number = 10;

public function TileSuppliesModelTest(methodName:String = null)
{
    super(methodName)
}

override protected function setUp():void
{
    super.setUp();
    instance = new TileSuppliesModel();
    instance.eventDispatcher = new EventDispatcher();
}

override protected function tearDown():void
{
    super.tearDown();
    instance = null;
}

public function test_set_supplyList():void
{
    var supplyList:Vector.<TileSupplyVO> = createSupplyList(5);

    instance.supplyList = supplyList;
    assertEqualsVectors("Set supplyList", supplyList, instance.supplyList);
}

public function test_addSupply_adds_a_supply_to_list():void
{
    var noOfItems:uint = 6;
    instance.supplyList = createSupplyList(noOfItems);
    instance.addSupply(ADDED_ID, ADDED_COLOR);
    var lastVO:TileSupplyVO = instance.supplyList[noOfItems];
    assertTrue("AddSupply adds appropriate supply to list",
                    voHasProperties(lastVO, ADDED_ID, ADDED_COLOR, 0));
}

protected function voHasProperties(vo1:TileSupplyVO, id:uint,
                              color:uint, count:Number):Boolean
{
    if (vo1.id != id) return false;
    if (vo1.color != color) return false;
    if (vo1.count != count) return false;

    return true;
```

```
}

protected function createSupplyList(length:uint):Vector.<TileSupplyVO>
{
    var supplyList:Vector.<TileSupplyVO> = new Vector.<TileSupplyVO>();

    var iLength:uint = length;
    for (var i:int = 0; i < iLength; i++)
    {
        var color:uint = 0x111111 * i;
        var count:Number = i * TILES_PER_INDEX;
        supplyList[i] = new TileSupplyVOSupport(i + 1);
    }
    return supplyList;
}

// more tests follow
}
```

Testing services

Interface mappings make it easy to test fails and errors too

Many services have a responsibility to inform the application when something has gone wrong—for example, that contact with the server has been lost and data wasn't able to be saved. If your service contains its own data paths it can be difficult to test that it behaves correctly in the face of an IOError, but if you inject your paths as dependencies you can configure your test service with a bad url very easily.

This example comes from a different application requiring a connection to a remote server in order to submit usage statistics:

Example 10-4. Dependency Injection makes it easy to switch urls and configurations to verify that our service deals with errors (AsUnit 3 tests)

```
public class StatsSubmissionServiceTest extends TestCase
{
private var instance:StatsSubmissionService;
private const LESSON_KEY:uint = 5;
private const CHECKPOINT:uint = 3;
private const SCRIPT_PATH_GOOD:String = 'http://appserver.com/submitStats.php5';
private const SCRIPT_PATH_BAD:String = 'http://dsajhdsahdjsak.dsa';
private const SESSION_KEY:uint = 10281;

public function StatsSubmissionServiceTest(methodName:String=null)
{
    super(methodName)
}

override protected function setUp():void {
    super.setUp();
    instance = new StatsSubmissionService();
    instance.eventDispatcher = new EventDispatcher();
    instance.sessionModel = new SessionModelSupport();
```

```
        instance.sessionModel.sessionKey = SESSION_KEY;
        instance.submitStatsScriptPath = SCRIPT_PATH_GOOD;
        instance.statsSubmissionXMLProcessor = new StatsSubmissionXMLProcessor();
}

override protected function tearDown():void {
        super.tearDown();
        instance = null;
}

public function test_fires_submission_completed_from_correct_url():void
{
        var handler:Function =
            addAsync(check_fires_submission_completed_from_correct_url, 10000);

        instance.eventDispatcher
            .addEventListener(StatsServiceEvent.SUBMISSION_COMPLETED, handler);

        instance.submitLessonCheckpoint(LESSON_KEY,CHECKPOINT);
}

private function check_fires_submission_completed_from_correct_url(
                                          e:StatsServiceEvent):void {
        assertEquals('event is correct type',
            StatsServiceEvent.SUBMISSION_COMPLETED, e.type);
}

public function test_dispatches_submission_failed_event_on_io_error():void
{
        var handler:Function =
            addAsync(check_dispatches_submission_failed_event_on_io_error, 3000);

        instance.eventDispatcher
            .addEventListener(StatsServiceEvent.SUBMISSION_FAILED, handler);

        instance.submitStatsScriptPath = SCRIPT_PATH_BAD;
        instance.submitLessonCheckpoint(LESSON_KEY,CHECKPOINT);
}

private function check_dispatches_submission_failed_event_on_io_error(
                                          e:StatsServiceEvent):void {
        assertEquals('correct type', StatsServiceEvent.SUBMISSION_FAILED, e.type);
}

public function test_check_submission_failed_event_if_script_fails():void
{
        var handler:Function =
            addAsync(check_check_submission_failed_event_if_script_fails, 8000);

        instance.eventDispatcher
            .addEventListener(StatsServiceEvent.SUBMISSION_FAILED, handler);

        instance.sessionModel = new BadSessionModelSupport();
        instance.submitLessonCheckpoint(LESSON_KEY, CHECKPOINT);
}
```

```
private function check_check_submission_failed_event_if_script_fails(
                                           e:StatsServiceEvent):void {
    assertEquals('correct type', StatsServiceEvent.SUBMISSION_FAILED, e.type);
}
```

Testing commands

Mock your dependencies and the IInjector

Most commands simply take the properties of the event that triggered them and then act appropriately on the model or service they've been injected with. If you're injecting against interfaces (and you should be!), this is where a good mocking framework comes in handy. Instead of supplying the dependencies using a real instance, you can use a 'mock'—a powerful and flexible technique for making tests easier to maintain and verifying how your class interacts with its dependencies.

In these tests we're using a mocking library called Mockolate—it's created by Drew Bourne and available at: *http://mockolate.org/*

There are different approaches to using mock objects (which also overlap with stubs and spies)—and it's too complex a subject to cover fully here, but hopefully if mocking is new to you, you'll get a feel for how powerful it can be based on our test examples.

A brief explanation of Mocking

Mocking is the practice of providing the class under test with one of its dependencies using a special object instead of just an instance of the class it would normally get when the application is running. You can create a mock manually, but there are also libraries available which do the bulk of that work for you—creating your mock at runtime.

There are three reasons why you'll want to use mocking: to avoid having to create an instance of an object that might be fiddly to bring to life (not just to save yourself the effort but to protect this test case from changes to how that object is constructed), to be able to specify and vary the responses an object gives when the class under test uses its API, and to spy on the class it's testing to check that it's doing its job exactly right.

In many cases you can use the mock created by your library without any further setup —but sometimes you'll want to customize it—for example to 'stub' the responses it gives to your class under test: "When you're asked for your selectedSupplyID, return 3".

If your command needs to make mappings on the Injector, you can also use mocking to verify these are being made correctly.

It might seem like some of your command code is too trivial to be worth testing, but a dodgy bit of command logic can create bugs that are hard to diagnose, so it's worth embracing mocking to get coverage of this part of your codebase.

Example 10-5. MosaicTool: UpdateDesignCommandTest.as uses mocking (by substituting real instances with objects created using Mockolate's nice() function) to verify that the command is carrying out a simple but important piece of control code correctly

```
public class UpdateDesignCommandTest extends TestCase
{
    protected var instance:UpdateDesignCommand;
    protected static const ROW:uint = 5;
    protected static const COLUMN:uint = 7;
    protected static const COLOR:uint = 0x333333;
    protected static const ID_WAS:uint = 2;
    protected static const ID_NOW:uint = 4;

    public function UpdateDesignCommandTest(methodName:String = null)
    {
        super(methodName)
    }

    // we override run in order to delay the test
    // until the mock classes have been prepared

    override public function run():void
    {
        var mockolateMaker:IEventDispatcher = prepare(IMosaicDesignModel,
                                                       ITileSuppliesModel);
        mockolateMaker.addEventListener(Event.COMPLETE, prepareCompleteHandler);
    }

    protected function prepareCompleteHandler(e:Event):void
    {
        IEventDispatcher(e.target).removeEventListener(Event.COMPLETE,
                                                       prepareCompleteHandler);
        super.run();
    }

    override protected function setUp():void
    {
        super.setUp();
        instance = new UpdateDesignCommand();
        instance.eventDispatcher = new EventDispatcher();

        // we supply the event that triggered this command
        instance.tileColorChangeEvent =
            new TileColorChangeEvent(TileColorChangeEvent.CHANGED, ROW, COLUMN, COLOR);

        // these are the classes with API that the command should be using
        instance.designModel = nice(IMosaicDesignModel);
        instance.tileSuppliesModel = nice(ITileSuppliesModel);

        // because the command uses the models to get values first
        // we need to 'stub' these functions to make sure they return something
        stub(instance.tileSuppliesModel).property("selectedSupplyID").returns(ID_NOW);
        stub(instance.designModel).method("changeTileColorAt").returns(ID_WAS);
    }
```

```
override protected function tearDown():void
{
    super.tearDown();
    instance = null;
}

public function testExecute_updates_model():void
{
    instance.execute();
    // checks that the method was run
    // and the arguments were passed in the right order
    verify(instance.designModel).method("changeTileColorAt")
            .args(equalTo(ROW), equalTo(COLUMN), equalTo(ID_NOW));
}

public function test_execute_updates_tileSupplies():void
{
    instance.execute();
    // checks that the method was run
    // and the arguments were passed in the right order
    verify(instance.tileSuppliesModel).method("switchTiles")
                    .args(equalTo(ID_WAS), equalTo(ID_NOW));
}
}
```

Testing mediators

Don't forget onRegister() **and** setViewComponent(view)
A mediator holds two references to your view—your own, strongly typed reference, and a more generally typed reference that it uses for the generic addViewListener function. So, your test needs to do the work of the mediatorMap by providing that generic reference to the viewComponent.

Your mediator just sits there, idly passing time, until onRegister has run, so normally you'll want to run this function in your setup, as well as providing the shared eventDispatcher.

Example 10-6. MosaicTool: SaveButtonMediatorTest.as setting up the mediator (AsUnit 3 test)

```
public function SaveButtonMediatorTest(methodName:String = null)
{
    super(methodName)
}

override protected function setUp():void
{
    super.setUp();
    instance = new SaveButtonMediator();
    instance.view = new SaveButton();
    instance.setViewComponent(instance.view);
    instance.eventDispatcher = new EventDispatcher();
    instance.onRegister();
}
```

Mediators generally only do two things—they translate view events into application events, and they translate application events into view API calls—so these are the two kinds of tests you'll be doing.

Testing that an event dispatched by the view results in the correct event being dispatched on the shared event dispatcher

This can be as simple as dispatching a `MouseEvent.CLICK` from the view itself and checking that the shared `eventDispatcher` dispatches the correct event. Manually dispatching clicks in your mediator tests soon gets repetitive, so you may want to make use of a helper for that—here it's done by a `UnitHelpers` class which simply dispatches the click on the object passed to the `clickItem` function.

Example 10-7. MosaicTool: SaveButtonMediatorTest.as verifying that a click on the view dispatches a SAVE_REQUESTED event (AsUnit 3 test)

```
public function test_click_on_view_dispatches_SAVE_REQUESTED_event():void
{
    var handler:Function =
        addAsync(check_click_on_view_dispatches_SAVE_REQUESTED_event, 50);
    instance.eventDispatcher
        .addEventListener(DesignSaveEvent.SAVE_REQUESTED, handler);

    UnitHelpers.clickItem(instance.view);
}

protected function check_click_on_view_dispatches_SAVE_REQUESTED_event(
                                                e:DesignSaveEvent):void
{
    assertEquals('event is correct type', DesignSaveEvent.SAVE_REQUESTED, e.type);
}
```

Testing that an event received on the shared event dispatcher results in an action on the view

You can do this using a concrete instance of your view, or you can mock the view using a mocking framework such as Mockolate or ASMock. Or you can make your own simple mock.

Example 10-8. MosaicTool: WorkspaceMediatorTest.as verifying that the mediator has used the view API using a concrete test (AsUnit 3 test)

```
public class WorkspaceMediatorTest extends TestCase
{
    protected var instance:WorkspaceMediator;
    protected static const NEW_COLOR:uint = 0x994488;

    public function WorkspaceMediatorTest(methodName:String = null)
    {
        super(methodName)
```

```
    }

    override protected function setUp():void
    {
        super.setUp();
        instance = new WorkspaceMediator();
        instance.view = new Workspace(10, 20);
        instance.setViewComponent(instance.view);
        instance.eventDispatcher = new EventDispatcher();
        instance.onRegister();
    }

    override protected function tearDown():void
    {
        super.tearDown();
        instance = null;
    }

    public function test_WorkspaceColorEvent_CHANGED_changes_color_on_view():void
    {
        var evt:WorkspaceColorEvent =
            new WorkspaceColorEvent(WorkspaceColorEvent.COLOR_CHANGED, NEW_COLOR);
        instance.eventDispatcher.dispatchEvent(evt);

        assertEquals("has passed color to view", NEW_COLOR,
                        UnitHelpers.getColorTransformOf(instance.view));
    }
}
```

In the next example we use Mockolate's `nice()` function to create a test double for an
instance of `Workspace`. This improves the test because we're able to check what the
workspace instance was asked to do, not what it actually did. If our workspace implementation introduced some internal logic for checking whether a colour was in range,
or applying a gradient fill that used the colour we passed, this test would still be useful,
where our original concrete test would now fail even though the change should be non-
breaking.

*Example 10-9. WorkspaceMediatorTest.as verifying that the mediator has used the view API using
a Mockolate mock (AsUnit 3 test)*

```
public class WorkspaceMediatorTest extends TestCase
{
    protected var instance:WorkspaceMediator;
    protected static const NEW_COLOR:uint = 0x994488;

    public function WorkspaceMediatorTest(methodName:String = null)
    {
        super(methodName)
    }

    override public function run():void{
        var mockolateMaker:IEventDispatcher = prepare(Workspace);
        mockolateMaker.addEventListener(Event.COMPLETE, prepareCompleteHandler);
    }
```

```
    private function prepareCompleteHandler(e:Event):void{
        IEventDispatcher(e.target)
            .removeEventListener(Event.COMPLETE, prepareCompleteHandler);
        super.run();
    }

    override protected function setUp():void
    {
        super.setUp();
        instance = new WorkspaceMediator();
        // we have to pass constructor args for mockolate to use for the Workspace
        instance.view = nice(Workspace, null, [10, 20]);
        instance.setViewComponent(instance.view);
        instance.eventDispatcher = new EventDispatcher();
        instance.onRegister();
    }

    override protected function tearDown():void
    {
        super.tearDown();
        instance = null;
    }

    public function test_WorkspaceColorEvent_CHANGED_changes_color_on_view():void
    {
        var evt:WorkspaceColorEvent =
            new WorkspaceColorEvent(WorkspaceColorEvent.COLOR_CHANGED, NEW_COLOR);
        instance.eventDispatcher.dispatchEvent(evt);

        verify(instance.view).setter("color").args(equalTo(NEW_COLOR));
    }
}
```

In the final example, we create our own mock, a class extending Workspace. Our simple mock overrides the normal behaviour of the Workspace class and allows us to read back the parameter we passed to the color setter.

Example 10-10. WorkspaceMediatorTest.as verifying that the mediator has used the view API using a simple custom mock(AsUnit 3 test)

```
public class WorkspaceMock extends Workspace
{
    protected var _color:uint;

    public function WorkspaceMock()
    {
        super(10, 20);
    }

    override public function set color(workspaceColor:uint):void
    {
        _color = workspaceColor;
    }
```

```
        override public function get color():uint
        {
            return _color;
        }
    }

    public class WorkspaceMediatorTest extends TestCase
    {
        protected var instance:WorkspaceMediator;
        protected static const NEW_COLOR:uint = 0x994488;

        public function WorkspaceMediatorTest(methodName:String = null)
        {
            super(methodName)
        }

        override protected function setUp():void
        {
            super.setUp();
            instance = new WorkspaceMediator();
            instance.view = new WorkspaceMock();
            instance.setViewComponent(instance.view);
            instance.eventDispatcher = new EventDispatcher();
            instance.onRegister();
        }

        override protected function tearDown():void
        {
            super.tearDown();
            instance = null;
        }

        public function test_WorkspaceColorEvent_CHANGED_changes_color_on_view():void
        {
            var evt:WorkspaceColorEvent =
                new WorkspaceColorEvent(WorkspaceColorEvent.COLOR_CHANGED, NEW_COLOR);
            instance.eventDispatcher.dispatchEvent(evt);

            assertEquals("has passed color to view", NEW_COLOR, instance.view.color);
        }
    }
```

This approach is a little more work than creating the mock using Mockolate, but more flexible than our original concrete test that relied on a real instance of Workspace. There are limitations on what can be mocked using a mocking framework. Unfortunately final methods can't be mocked which means automatically generating mocks for classes extending UIComponent isn't possible. Vector return types can also cause difficulties. In both these situations, rolling your own mock class is a good alternative.

 If your mediator also overrides onRemove then don't forget to run this in your test teardown, so you don't leave any listeners hanging around, preventing garbage collection. You can run preRemove (where the mediator's eventMap is cleaned up) if you want to, but it's not necessary.

CHAPTER 11

Power-ups

Used as described so far, Robotlegs is a pareto solution: the 20% of the solutions that can fix 80% of your problems. In a complex application you'll probably run into some of the problems that the most basic implementation of Robotlegs doesn't tackle. Some of these problems can be fixed using the less well-used parts of the Robotlegs framework itself, others are better solved by pulling in extra libraries.

Still, we regularly find that problems brought to the Robotlegs forum can be solved using conventional OO techniques—so, while the power-ups we're covering here are useful, don't forget that most of your OO understanding still applies: Just Code Normal.

Bootstraps can break up fat contexts

Even a small application can require a large number of injection, command and mediator mappings—so your `startup()` function can quickly grow to dozens of lines, with your context importing scores of classes. An antidote to this is to use 'BootstrapCommands'—commands which run just once during your application's startup, with the relevant wiring for your app spread across several focused commands.

```
// in your Context startup function
commandMap.mapEvent(ContextEvent.STARTUP_COMPLETE, MapServicesCommand);

public class MapServicesCommand extends Command
{
    override public function execute():void
    {
        injector.mapSingletonOf(IMosaicConfigLoadingService,
                                MosaicConfigSolLoadingService);
        injector.mapSingletonOf(IMosaicConfigSavingService,
                                MosaicConfigSolSavingService);
    }
}
```

You'll want to make sure these commands extend the Robotlegs base `Command` class, as you'll need access to the injector, command map, mediator map and so on.

Some developers break up their bootstrapping by type: `MapModels`, `MapServices`, `MapMediators`, `MapCommands`. Others prefer to separate by feature, for example `MapGameStartup`, `MapGamePlay`, `MapMenus`.

A final option is to 'Just Code Normal'—you can use an ordinary class to just break up your mappings into smaller pieces, and just call these directly in your context— passing in the injector, mediator map, command map and so on as needed, either to the constructor or to a function. (You could even use package level functions if you're familiar with them).

Example 11-1. The Mosaic Design Tool makes use of conventional objects for mappings

```
public class BootstrapServices
{
    public function BootstrapServices(injector:IInjector)
    {
        injector.mapSingletonOf(IMosaicConfigLoadingService,
                                MosaicConfigSolLoadingService);
        injector.mapSingletonOf(IMosaicConfigSavingService,
                                MosaicConfigSolSavingService);
        //... etc
    }
}

public class MosaicContext extends Context
{
    public function MosaicContext(contextView:DisplayObjectContainer)
    {
        super(contextView, true);
    }

    override public function startup():void
    {
        new BootstrapConfigValues(injector);
        new BootstrapModels(injector);
        new BootstrapServices(injector);
        new BootstrapCommands(commandMap);
        new BootstrapTileSupplyCommands(commandMap);
        new BootstrapClasses(injector);
        new BootstrapViewMediators(mediatorMap);

        addRootView();
        // and we're done
        super.startup();
    }

    protected function addRootView():void
    {
        var tileFactory:ITileFactory = new TileFactory(20, 0x333333);
        var mainView:MosaicToolView = new MosaicToolView(tileFactory, 150);
        contextView.addChild(mainView);
    }
}
```

The ContextEvents help keep control

You can wire your bootstrap commands to the event that is automatically dispatched by the startup() function in the Robotlegs Context class that your context extends: ContextEvent.STARTUP_COMPLETE

```
// in startup
commandMap.mapEvent(ContextEvent.STARTUP_COMPLETE, MapGameStartup);
commandMap.mapEvent(ContextEvent.STARTUP_COMPLETE, MapGamePlay);
commandMap.mapEvent(ContextEvent.STARTUP_COMPLETE, MapMenus);
```

There's also another context event: ContextEvent.STARTUP, which you can dispatch from your context (on the shared eventDispatcher) yourself if you need to run your bootstraps in two batches. This is rare, but perhaps you need to read a variable from a local SharedObject and then use that to configure how your application is wired up.

Alternatively, you can dispatch a custom event of your own when you're ready for your bootstrap commands to run:

```
// in startup
commandMap.mapEvent(AppEvent.INITIALIZED, MapGameStartup);
commandMap.mapEvent(AppEvent.INITIALIZED, MapGamePlay);
commandMap.mapEvent(AppEvent.INITIALIZED, MapMenus);

dispatch(new ApplicationEvent(AppEvent.INITIALIZED));
```

Tag methods with [PostConstruct] to run them after injection is complete

Whichever approach you use for your injection (property, setter or constructor injection) you'll find that it's not possible to do work in the constructor of your class.

With property and setter injection you'll run into null errors, as the dependencies are only fulfilled after the constructor has run.

With constructor injection, a bug in the flash player means that the class has to be instantiated before the describeType information for the constructor is available. The injector needs this information to know what to inject into the constructor. This means that the injector has to create and then dispose of an instance of this class, just to find out how to instantiate it. As a result, doing work in the constructor is a bad idea.

This problem only affects constructor injection—property and setter injection don't require the creation of a disposable instance. But, regardless, you can't do work in the constructor of a class that has injections of any kind.

So, in order to have some functionality run as soon as the object is created *and* has all its dependencies fulfilled, you can use the [PostConstruct] metadata tag to label methods (which must be public) which the injector should kick into action.

If you need to have more than one method run in a specific order, there are two options:

- Use [PostConstruct] on an init() method to run the other methods in order
- Add multiple [PostConstruct(order=1)], [PostConstruct(order=2)] etc tags to label the methods in order

The major weaknesses of custom metadata are that it's not compiler safe, and it requires the injector to be present in order to process it. If your object only has one dependency then you might prefer to use a trigger on a setter injection method to kick things off:

```
[Inject]
public function set targetFolder(folder:File)
{
    _folder = folder;
    initMonitoring();
}
```

If you override a method marked [PostConstruct] you'll need to add it in the subclass too

If you extend a class with a [PostConstruct] method and you override that method, the compiler will use the describe-type data from the subclass and not the superclass, so it won't know about the original [PostConstruct] tag. You need to tag the subclass method with [PostConstruct] too. If you're working on a class which includes [PostConstruct] functions that others are likely to override, give some thought to whether there's a more fool-proof way to achieve the same end result.

Use Signals between complex views and their mediators

AS3Signals is a library by Robert Penner which provides an alternative to AS3 Events for communicating between objects. There are a number of reasons why Robert created the library, and the main advantages it provides are:

- A Signal is a property of a class, which means you can define it on the interface for that class.
- You can only listen to a Signal if the class has that Signal as a property—unlike events, where you can listen for a TimerEvent on an Elephant if you want to.
- When you create a Signal, you define the number and type of arguments this Signal is going to dispatch.
- When you add a handler to a Signal, the Signal does some checking to make sure your handler expects the right number of arguments.
- When you dispatch a Signal, it validates the data values you're dispatching against the types it expected to send.
- You can 'addOnce' to a signal—so the handler is unmapped as soon as the Signal has fired.
- You can 'removeAll' from a signal—unmapping all the handlers in one go.

- Signals themselves aren't strings, they are objects, and can be strongly typed. Unlike AS3 Events, which rely on string constants.

Signals are, unsurprisingly, faster to dispatch than events. And because they're strong typed objects you can inject them in your application. You can find out more about Signals at *https://github.com/robertpenner/as3-signals*

A really neat use of AS3Signals is to expose 'click' signals for several buttons on the same view, without having to expose the buttons themselves. If you expose the actual buttons, with a getter, then the button is vulnerable to being moved, having its alpha changed, even having its event dispatching switched off. Of course, no sensible coder would do this, but still, it's a lot to expose when really you just want to allow an interested object to find out when a specific button has been clicked.

Using AS3Signals to dispatch specific clicks for different buttons on a view is a very simple implementation that avoids having to expose view parts to mediators:

Example 11-2. Mosaic Designer:TileSupplyDetailView.as and TileSupplyDetailViewMediator.as—without signals

```
public class TileSupplyDetailView extends BaseColorSelectorView
{
    // currently the TileSupplyDetailView exposes its buttons:
    public function get radioButton():RadioButton
    {
        return _radioButton;
    }

    public function get deleteButton():Sprite
    {
        return _deleteButton;
    }
    //...
}

public class TileSupplyDetailViewMediator extends Mediator
{
    [Inject]
    public var view:TileSupplyDetailView;

    override public function onRegister():void
    {
        eventMap.mapListener(view.deleteButton, MouseEvent.CLICK,
                            dispatchDeletionRequest, MouseEvent);
        eventMap.mapListener(view.radioButton, MouseEvent.CLICK,
                            dispatchSupplySelected, MouseEvent);
        addViewListener(ColorChangeEvent.CHANGED,
                            dispatchColorChange, ColorChangeEvent);
        addContextListener(TileSupplyEvent.QUANTITY_CHANGED,
                            updateCount, TileSupplyEvent);
    }

    protected function dispatchDeletionRequest(e:MouseEvent):void
```

```
    {
        var evt:TileSupplyEvent =
            new TileSupplyEvent(TileSupplyEvent.SUPPLY_DELETION_REQUESTED, view.id,
                                                    view.selectedColor, 0);
        dispatch(evt);
    }

    protected function dispatchSupplySelected(e:MouseEvent):void
    {
        var evt:TileSupplyEvent =
            new TileSupplyEvent(TileSupplyEvent.SUPPLY_SELECTED, view.id,
                                                    view.selectedColor, 0);
        dispatch(evt);
    }
    //...
}
```

Example 11-3. Mosaic Designer: using Signals to differentiate clicks while hiding their sources in TileSupplyDetailView.as and TileSupplyDetailViewMediator.as

```
public class TileSupplyDetailView extends BaseColorSelectorView
{
    // we can use signals to relay the clicks without
    // exposing the buttons
    public function get selected():Signal
    {
        return _selectedSignal;
    }

    public function get deleted():Signal
    {
        return _deletedSignal;
    }

    protected function configureButtons():void
    {
        _radioButton.addEventListener(MouseEvent.CLICK, relaySelected);
        _deleteButton.addEventListener(MouseEvent.CLICK, relayDeleted);
    }

    protected function relaySelected(e:MouseEvent):void
    {
        _selectedSignal.dispatch();
    }

    protected function relayDeleted(e:MouseEvent):void
    {
        _deletedSignal.dispatch();
    }
    //...
}

public class TileSupplyDetailViewMediator extends Mediator
{
    [Inject]
    public var view:TileSupplyDetailView;
```

```
override public function onRegister():void
{
    // instead of attaching to the buttons, we can add listeners to the signals
    view.selected.add(dispatchSupplySelected);
    view.selected.add(dispatchDeletionRequest);
    addViewListener(ColorChangeEvent.CHANGED, dispatchColorChange, ColorChangeEvent);
    addContextListener(TileSupplyEvent.QUANTITY_CHANGED, updateCount,
                                                    TileSupplyEvent);
}

// the handlers are the same but don't require the event argument
protected function dispatchDeletionRequest(e:MouseEvent):void
{
    var evt:TileSupplyEvent =
        new TileSupplyEvent(TileSupplyEvent.SUPPLY_DELETION_REQUESTED, view.id,
                                            view.selectedColor, 0);
    dispatch(evt);
}

protected function dispatchSupplySelected(e:MouseEvent):void
{
    var evt:TileSupplyEvent =
        new TileSupplyEvent(TileSupplyEvent.SUPPLY_SELECTED, view.id,
                                            view.selectedColor, 0);
    dispatch(evt);
}
//...
}
```

But we can do better—rather than listen directly to the signals, use the `SignalMap` and `SignalMediator` to get auto-cleanup parity with the eventMap version. You then register for the different signals like this:

```
override public function onRegister():void
{
    // add normally
    addToSignal(view.deleteRequested, someHandler);

    // add once
    addOnceToSignal(view.submit, submitHandler);
}
```

Like the `EventMap`, the `SignalMap` cleans up all those listeners when the view leaves the stage. The Signals registered can be properties of the view, or they can be injected 'Signaltons' (A Signal which is also mapped as a singleton in your injector).

Modular and multiple-context Robotlegs

'Modular' Robotlegs can refer to a number of different setups—you might have a Robotlegs shell which loads Robotlegs Flex Modules, or a non-Robotlegs shell which loads Robotlegs swfs that aren't Flex Modules, or you might compile multiple Robotlegs contexts into a single swf. The good news is that developers have had great success using all of these approaches.

Communicating between contexts in Robotlegs can be as simple as sharing an event dispatcher. But if you want to share injections and instances between contexts then you need the Robotlegs Modular Utilities: *https://github.com/joelhooks/robotlegs-utilities-Modular*

Deep exploration of the Modular approach to Robotlegs is out of scope for this book, but you'll find a link to an example in the repository and several people have done excellent tutorials covering modular Robotlegs on their blogs. The following is only a brief outline to help you decide whether Modular Robotlegs is of use to you.

ModuleEventDispatcher and child injectors make it work

Cast your mind back to the very beginning of this book. We summarised Robotlegs as a *Communication and Cooperation* framework. The same challenges that we face in our architecture in a single context are echoed when we try to bring contexts together:

Communicating between contexts
> Keeping each context informed of events that might concern it occurring in other contexts.
>
> Robotlegs Modular achieves this by giving each module a reference to the same instance of a ModuleEventDispatcher—an event dispatcher targeted at distributing messages throughout the application rather than just local to this module.

Cooperating across contexts
> Allowing an object in one context to cooperate with an object in another context *directly.*
>
> Robotlegs Modular achieves this using *child injectors*. Instead of each module context creating its own self-contained injector, there is a single 'parent' injector for the application, and each module context is passed a child injector created by this parent injector.
>
> Injection rules can be shared between the parent context and the child contexts. For example, mapping a singleton of an interface in the shell context allows all the child modules to make use of this rule, and receive the same instance in every child module.

The Modular Utilities contain special 'modular' versions of the command map and mediator, allowing you to differentiate between dispatching and responding to events on the between-modules event dispatcher and an individual context's internal shared event dispatcher.

Sharing message dispatchers and injection rules is surprisingly straightforward. From a technical perspective, if you can build a single-context Robotlegs application then you can build a multi-context one by mastering only a few extra principles. The ob-

---

stacles people run into are those affecting any multi-swf project: application domains, security domains, dividing responsibilities between modules, timing issues and so on.

Don't let that put you off though! Robotlegs actually helps with many of the difficulties of multi-swf development. Being able to inject instances against interfaces allows you to avoid compiling implementations (the classes with the actual code) into multiple swfs, resulting in fewer recompiles when you make changes. The ease with which you can switch the classes used to fulfil injections makes testing modules in isolation much less labour intensive than when using manual dependency injection. Module mediators (that can relay messages from the inter-module dispatcher to the local one) make it possible to build services and models which can be used in single and multiple context applications just as easily.

Extend Robotlegs with utilities and add-ons

The core Robotlegs framework aims to solve 80% of your application-wiring related problems, but you can extend the range of possibilities with various utilities and plugins for the system. Most of these utilities have been created by framework users rather than the Robotlegs main team. Some replace parts of the core system but the majority are add-ons. The list is constantly growing, but here's a selection of utilities available today —all of them hosted on github:

- **Alternative event maps**
  —Relaxed Event Map (*https://github.com/Stray/robotlegs-utilities-RelaxedEvent Map*)—an event map that beats race conditions
- **Alternative command maps**
  —Signal Command Map (*https://github.com/joelhooks/signals-extensions-Com mandSignal*)—commands triggered by signals instead of events
  —Macrobot (*https://github.com/Aaronius/robotlegs-utilities-Macrobot*)—execute batches of commands in sequence or in parallel
  —Guarded Command Map (*https://github.com/Stray/GuardedCommandMap*)— abstracts the conditions for running a command from the command itself
  —Guarded Signal Command Map (*https://github.com/neilmanuell/signals-exten sions-CommandSignal/tree/master/src/org/robotlegs/base*)—a signal driven command map with abstraction of conditions for running the command from the command itself
  —Option Command Map (*https://github.com/Stray/robotlegs-utilities-OptionCom mandMap*)—allows specific commands to be mapped against generic events at runtime, useful for option menus
  —Compound Command Map (*https://github.com/Stray/robotlegs-utilities-Com poundCommandMap*)—maps a command to a combination of events

- Deferred Command Queue (*https://github.com/Stray/robotlegs-utilities-Defer redCommandQueue*)—queues commands and runs them consecutively
- UndoableCommands and HistoryController (*https://github.com/secoif/robot legs-utilities-UndoableCommand*)—undo, redo, rewind, fastforward and step through your command history

- **Alternative mediators and mediator maps**
  - View Interface Mediator Map (*https://github.com/piercer/robotlegs-extensions -ViewInterfaceMediatorMap*)—a mediator map that maps to interfaces of views
  - Lazy Mediator Map (*https://github.com/wrobel221/robotlegs-utilities-LazyMe diator*)—a mediator map which relies on a custom event instead of `ADDED_TO_STAGE` in order to improve performance
  - Signal Mediator and Signal Map (*https://github.com/Stray/robotlegs-utilities-Sig nalMediator*)—provides automatic clean up of signal listeners added in mediators

- **Control/flow utilities**
  - AS3 Navigator (*https://github.com/epologee/navigator-as3*)—an extensive library for managing state changes, history, swfAddress integration and much more, with Robotlegs integration examples
  - State Machine (*https://github.com/joelhooks/robotlegs-utilities-StateMachine*)— a Robotlegs port of the PureMVC Finite State Machine (event driven)
  - Robotlegs Signal State Machine (*https://github.com/AS3StateMachine/AS3-Sig nal-StateMachine-for-Robotlegs*)—a guarded state machine driven by AS3 Signals

- **Modular application utilities**
  - Robotlegs Modular Utilities (*https://github.com/joelhooks/robotlegs-utilities -Modular*)—helper classes for building modular applications with Robotlegs

- **Other frameworks**
  - Gaia—Robotlegs example (*https://github.com/kyoji2/RobotGaiaAnt*)—an example application integrating Gaia, Robotlegs and Signals
  - Away3D Robotlegs integration (*https://github.com/PaulTondeur/Robotlegs -Away3D-Extension*)—helper classes (3D context, 3D mediator, 3D mediator map and more) for working with Away3D and Robotlegs together

- **Other utilities**
  - Oil (*https://github.com/darscan/robotlegs-extensions-Oil*)—Shaun Smith's personal Robotlegs utils, including 'promises' for working with asynchronous services
  - Asset Loader (*https://github.com/Matan/AssetLoader/*)—a Signals driven asset loading library that integrates well with Robotlegs

---

ViewMap—injection for your views

The ViewMap provides auto DI for your views. Like the mediator map, it listens for Event.ADDED_TO_STAGE on the context view, and then checks to see whether the view that has been added has been mapped in the context using:

viewMap.mapType(SomeView);

Alternatively, you can request injection on all the views in a package using the package name:

viewMap.mapPackage('com.example.view.characters');

When the view map finds that a view that has been added to the stage is one of the mapped types, or comes from one of the mapped packages, it passes this view to the injector to have its dependencies fulfilled.

In reality, injection into your views is problematic, and we don't recommend that you take this approach unless you have a very specific purpose for it. Generally, the kinds of applications—usually games—that would benefit from view injection are also the applications where performance is most important, and there are much more performant ways to pass dependencies to view classes—for example by instantiating them via a factory.

Another approach is to use a 'double-decoupled' static reference—basically a resource locator where the resource is configured in your startup or at runtime by a command. For example, if you wanted to be able to quickly switch out stylesheets for your characters:

```
public class CharacterSkinLookup
{
    public function setSkin(characterSkin:ICharacterSkin)
    {
        _characterSkin = characterSkin;
    }

    public static function lookupCharacterSkin(viewClass:Class)
    {
        return _characterSkin.lookupSkinFor(viewClass);
    }
}

public class PopulateCharacterSkinCommand()
{
    [Inject]
    public var styleLookup:CharacterSkinLookup;

    [Inject]
    public var skinLoadEvent:SkinEvent;

    override public function execute():void
    {
        styleLookup.setSkin(skinLoadEvent.loadedSkin);
```

```
    }
}

public class BossCharacterView extends CharacterView
{
    public function BossCharacterView():void
    {
        applySkin(CharacterSkinLookup.lookupCharacterSkin(BossCharacterView));
    }
}
```

 Never use the view map in combination with the mediator map—the performance hit from running two sets of interrogation of objects arriving on and leaving the stage for every `Event.ADDED_TO_STAGE` and `Event.REMOVED_TO_STAGE` is horrible.

Mediator map performance

The automagic creation that the mediator map does is reliant upon listening to every single `Event.ADDED_TO_STAGE` and `Event.REMOVED_FROM_STAGE` event that is dispatched by your contextView. In some applications that's a handful of events, but in any application where views are regularly arriving on or leaving the stage, you can experience a real drag on performance.

It's possible to switch this listening on and off using the mediator map's `enabled` property, by accessing the mediator map in a command. For example, if your application was a game, and you wanted to use mediation of the UI for the game start, and between levels, but not during levels when views are being added to and removed from stage rapidly, you could deactivate the mediator map at the start of each level and then activate it again when the level ends:

```
public class StartLevelCommand extends Command
{
    override public function execute():void
    {
        mediatorMap.enabled = false;
    }
}

public class EndLevelCommand extends Command
{
    override public function execute():void
    {
        // careful of race conditions - this needs to happen before
        // your menu items start to hit the stage
        mediatorMap.enabled = true;
    }
}
```

If you're very worried about mediator map performance then we recommend that you check out the `LazyMediatorMap` utility as an alternative.

Troubleshooting tips

While we're always happy to answer questions on the forum, if your problem falls into the category of things that can happen to any Robotlegs project, this reference is probably the fastest way to get a solution. If you don't find the answer here, or your problem is more closely tied to the specific details of your application, hit the forums and the community will help you out.

Problem: Injection doesn't occur

This is probably the most common problem that developers working with Robotlegs for the first time experience. The usual causes are:

- Broken injection point declaration
- Metadata is being stripped by the compiler
- Instantiating an object with injected dependencies using new
- Injected properties are null in constructor

Broken injection point declaration

Because the Flash/Flex compiler can't validate custom metadata, an error in your injection point you won't produce a compiler error, you'll just find that the injection hasn't happened and the value is null.

This is what a healthy injected dependency looks like:

```
[Inject]
public var someValue:SomeType;
```

What's gone wrong?

Did you make the property public? This won't work because the injector can't access the property to set it:

```
[Inject]
private var someValue:SomeType;
```

Metadata is case sensitive, so none of these will work:

```
[inject] [INJECT] [InJect]
```

A semi-colon between the metadata and the variable breaks the relationship, so this won't work:

```
[Inject];
public var someValue:SomeType;
```

Metadata is being stripped by the compiler

See "You need to tell the compiler to include the injection metadata" on page 33.

Instantiating an object with injected dependencies using new

Injection isn't magic! It's a very neat factory approach to creating objects, and unless you ask the factory to create your object, or to process it after you've instantiated it, injection can't happen.

So, if you're creating your object using new you need to feed it through the injector. But, if you've got the injector at hand, you'd be better to ask the Injector to create it and fulfil its dependencies all in one go:

```
var thing:Thing = injector.instantiate(Thing);
```

Injected properties are null in constructor

If you're not using constructor injection, the dependencies you're hoping to have the injector provide aren't going to be provided until after the constructor has finished running. The order in which the process happens is:

1. Cache is checked to see if we've met this type before
2. Cached or fresh type description is interrogated to see what injection points exist
3. new Thing(...) with constructor injection requirements fulfilled
4. Property and setter injections fulfilled

Don't be tempted to get around this using constructor injection—unfortunately the injector has to create a disposable instance of a class (just once) to find out what injections it expects, so you shouldn't do work in the constructor either way.

Instead, you can use the [PostConstruct] tag. For more info see "Tag methods with [PostConstruct] to run them after injection is complete" on page 105.

Problem: Things work for a while and then mysteriously stop

Did you remember to hang on to your context? If you do this, your context, and usually everything in it, will eventually be garbage collected:

```
var unstableContext:SomeContext = new SomeContext(this);
```

So always make sure to hang on to your context in a property:

```
protected var _context:MosaicContext;

public function mosaictool()
{
    _context = new MosaicContext(this);
}
```

Problem: Event dispatch does not work as expected

Make sure you override the clone() method of your custom event class. Events cannot be re-dispatched without doing so – even non-bubbling events. It is considered best practice when creating custom events to override clone().

Problem: Mediator isn't running onRegister

First, check all of the following:

- Have you created a mapping for this view-mediator pair?
- Is your mapping against the actual concrete type of this view? The mediatorMap doesn't look at the superclasses or interfaces of the views hitting the stage, it only looks at the actual class
- Is your view being added to the stage? The mediator onRegister() method runs after the view has landed on stage. It's possible to addChild(view) without the view actually being added to the stage, if the parent is not on stage
- If your view is definitely mapped to the mediator and is definitely being added to the stage: has your view hit the stage *before* the mapping was made?

Make mediator mappings from the inside out

Generally you should aim to list your mediator mappings from the inside out – map the most deeply nested view first, and your contextView last. This ensures that if you have an init() function in your parent view that adds the internal children, and is triggered by the onRegister of the parent mediator, all the child mappings will already have been made before this code runs, and your views won't hit the stage before their mappings have been made.

```
mediatorMap.mapView(GreatGrandchildA, GreatGrandchildAMediator);
mediatorMap.mapView(GreatGrandchildB, GreatGrandchildBMediator);
mediatorMap.mapView(Grandchild, GrandchildMediator);
mediatorMap.mapView(ChildA, ChildAMediator);
mediatorMap.mapView(AppContext, AppContextMediator);
```

Problem: Handlers in the mediator are running repeatedly

Check:

- Have you added a listener directly to the shared `eventDispatcher` or view, instead of using the `eventMap`?
- If you're injecting Signals into this view, have you used `SignalMediator` and `SignalMap` to make sure your listeners are removed automatically?

The event map is cleaned up automatically when the mediator is destroyed (when the view leaves the stage). If you map listeners directly then they can persist, and each time your view hits the stage a new mediator will be created for it, but these mediators won't be garbage collected when they are destroyed. Depending on how many times your view leaves and rejoins the stage you could see an increasing number of traces from a handler that has been added directly.

So avoid doing this:

```
view.addEventListener(MouseEvent.CLICK, dispatchSaveRequestedEvent);
```

And instead do this:

```
addViewListener(MouseEvent.CLICK, dispatchSaveRequestedEvent, MouseEvent);
```

And if you're listening to a sub-component, make use of the eventMap directly:

```
eventMap.mapListener(view.yesBtn, MouseEvent.CLICK, dispatchYes, MouseEvent);
```

Error: Injector missing rule for X

Try not to get cross at the injector when it tells you it can't find the rule for this injection point—at least it's giving you a specific error rather than just leaving you at the mercy of the AS3 'null thing, sorry, won't tell you what was null' error that we all love so much.

This error means that you haven't supplied the injector with a rule for this type *at the time when it tried to make the injection.* Maybe you haven't made the mapping at all, maybe you've made a small mistake in your mapping, or maybe it's a *race conditions* problem—the injector is trying to make the injection before you've made the mapping.

Missing injection mapping

The injector needs to be provided with a rule about how to fulfil each injection. If you have an [Inject] point, you must have a corresponding mapping on the injector, either directly through the injector mapping methods or through the commandMap (which defines an injection rule for each event you map) and mediatorMap (which defines an injection rule for each view you map). If you feel like you're staring at the injection mapping right there, check whether your problem is actually *inconsistent* injection mapping.

Inconsistent injection mapping

Remember that if you've mapped a class using `mapSingletonOf` then you must inject using the first parameter and not the concrete class.

```
injector.mapSingletonOf(ISomeType, SomeType);
injector.mapSingletonOf(BaseSomeType, SpecialSomeType);
```

So, these injections will be fine:

```
[Inject]
public var someValue:ISomeType;

[Inject]
public var someOtherValue:BaseSomeType;
```

But these injections will produce an injection error:

```
[Inject]
public var someValue:SomeType;

[Inject]
public var someOtherValue:SpecialSomeType;
```

Warning: Duplicate mapping in the injector

Later versions of Swiftsuspenders will complain if you repeat a mapping that it already has an entry for, so the following would produce an error:

```
injector.mapSingletonOf(ISomeType, SomeType);
injector.mapValue(ISomeType, new SpecialType(6));
```

This is easy to spot if the mappings are consecutive or even close together, but harder to spot if you're making your mapping in a command later on. To avoid seeing this error, you should explicitly undo the existing mapping before you make the new one.

```
injector.mapSingletonOf(ISomeType, SomeType);
// likely in some other class - perhaps a command or factory
injector.unmap(ISomeType);
mapValue(ISomeType, new SpecialType(6));
```

If you are replacing a value regularly you won't need to unmap it the first time you set it, so you can use `hasMapping` to check whether it is necessary.

```
if( injector.hasMapping(ISomeType) )
{
    injector.unmap(ISomeType);
}
mapValue(ISomeType, new SpecialType(6));
```

This warning doesn't actually prevent the new mapping from being made, it's only there to advise you that something out of the ordinary has happened, in case it was accidental.

Error: Call to a possibly undefined method X

Among other reasons, this error could be the result of not following the AS3 naming conventions for packages, classes, methods, variables, and so on.

For example, can you spot the mistake here? (The answer is in this footnote*)

```
package controller
{
    import model.MyModel;
    import org.robotlegs.mvcs.Command;

    public class MyCommand extends Command
    {
        [Inject]
        public var model:MyModel;

        override public function execute():void
        {
            model.myMethod();
        }
    }
}
```

would result in:

1. Error 1180: Call to a possibly undefined method myMethod
2. Warning 3599: Definition name is the same as an imported package name

This ambiguity produces errors when the compiler tries and fails to find the myMethod() function in the model package. Of course you intended it to look within the MyModel class.

The solution is simple: package your classes properly!

This is the safest: domain.project.area.model.SomeModel

Where to get more help

Robotlegs was, from the outset, intended to break the "Not for noobs" convention that existed around AS3 frameworks. The forum is friendly and responsive, and we're enthusiastic about helping you to get going with Robotlegs, as well as answering more advanced questions. So, don't be shy—if you have a problem or a question find us at:

Our forum: knowledge.robotlegs.org (*http://knowledge.robotlegs.org*)

Twitter—@jhooks (*http://www.twitter.com/jhooks*), @stray_and_ruby (*http://www.twitter.com/stray_and_ruby*), @darscan (*http://www.twitter.com/darscan*), @tschneidereit (*http://www.twitter.com/tscheidereit*)

---

* There is an import package called 'model' and also a variable called 'model'.

Swiftsuspenders: The power behind the Robotlegs Injector

When Robotlegs was first created, the intention was to leave the choice of which actual injector to use to process metadata to the end user.

The out-of-the-box solution uses an injection container called *Swiftsuspenders*, created by the brilliant Till Schneidereit. As it turns out, we like the Swiftsuspenders injector so much that it's unlikely that anybody is actually using anything different, and on a practical level Swiftsuspenders *is* the Robotlegs Injector, and we expect the two to continue to evolve together.

What does Swiftsuspenders actually do?

Swiftsuspenders essentially does two things: it interrogates classes (using the AS3 reflection capabilities) and it manages the supply of objects to fulfil dependencies using the rules you set up on the injector.

The challenge of automated DI is that AS3 reflection isn't very efficient, so squeezing every last drop of performance out of the process is difficult but important, and this is where the Swiftsuspenders injector earns its plaudits.

Swiftsuspenders uses caching to limit the number of times each class is described, and does all object instantiation and description as lazily as possible—a class won't be described, or created, until an instance is required. If you have a reason for wanting your mapped objects to be created and described eagerly, you can deliberately instantiate the class after each mapping (making sure any of its injections have already been mapped):

```
// instructs the injector about how to make this mapping
injector.mapSingletonOf(IEventSpy, ParanoidEventSpy);
// returns the instance, so our ParanoidEventSpy would now be up and running
injector.getInstance(IEventSpy);
```

We think limited metadata is a good thing

The Swiftsuspenders injector processes only two metadata tags: [Inject] and [PostConstruct]

The more the Robotlegs team have considered it, the more we've come to the belief that limiting the range of custom metadata used by the framework is a good idea—after all, those of us who used to code in ActionScript 1 understand just how much of an advantage compile-time checking is. The more we introduce into our code that the compiler can't verify, the more bugs there are that have to be hunted down while our software is actually running.

In addition, because when you run a unit test you're usually operating outside of the injector, metadata problems are difficult to eliminate in testing (except for end-to-end tests).

The more custom metadata is relied upon in your application, the less chance there is that your code will be reusable outside the framework and metadata processor it has been customised for.

Finally, the more custom metadata you use, the more you're asking of the programmers who maintain your software in future. Your codebase becomes tightly coupled to you as a programmer as well as that metadata processor you're using—Joel likes to joke that this is job security, but if you want to enjoy the freedom of knowing you could hand a project over to somebody else, then good programmer-codebase decoupling is vital.

About the Authors

Joel Hooks is a Flash Platform developer with experience in Actionscript 3, Flex, and Python. Joel spent the first 13 years of his professional career as a 3d animator and graphic designer working on computer-based training applications from that perspective. His interest in programming goes as far back as "TELL TURTLE" and he has always been interested in the technological challenges related to developing software and making work a little bit easier. With the introduction of Actionscript 3, Joel finally found a platform that allows him to architect useful tools while fully leveraging his experience as a visual artist. Joel is passionate about technology and enjoys exploring the landscape of frameworks, libraries, and tools that make his work constantly fun and challenging. Joel currently resides in Fort Worth and works as a Flex consultant for Universal Mind providing clients with oodles of clean code and a focus on test-driven development solutions. Joel can be found blogging on various Flex development topics at *http://joelhooks.com*. Outside of developing software tools, Joel owns a photography studio (*http://visualempathy.com*) with his wife, who also collaborates on the raising and nurturing of his four home-educated children aged 4 to 13.

Lindsey Fallow (aka Stray) has spent the past decade exploring science and technology as a writer, software developer, and television personality. Following an undergraduate degree in Manufacturing Engineering, she fronted a science show for 8–12 year-olds on Disney, and went on to become a reporter & Associate Producer for Tomorrow's World (the BBC's #1 prime-time UK science and technology show) from 1998-2002. She's stood on the top of the Golden Gate bridge, fed sharks, filmed brain surgery, flown in military planes, and been bitten by a baby tiger, but is the most excited by far when her 16-year-old stepson 'gets' new math concepts. A Flash developer since Flash 4, Stray blogs on ActionScript, test driven development and the programmer's brain at *http://www.xxcoder.net/*. She is a core contributor to the Robotlegs framework, and actively pushing the ActionScript community to aspire to excellence through the try{harder} collaborative-learning format.

Colophon

The animal on the cover of *ActionScript Developer's Guide to Robotlegs* is an oyster catcher.

The cover image is from *Riverside*. The cover font is Adobe ITC Garamond. The text font is Linotype Birka; the heading font is Adobe Myriad Condensed; and the code font is LucasFont's TheSansMonoCondensed.

Get even more for your money.

Join the O'Reilly Community, and register the O'Reilly books you own. It's free, and you'll get:

- $4.99 ebook upgrade offer
- 40% upgrade offer on O'Reilly print books
- Membership discounts on books and events
- Free lifetime updates to ebooks and videos
- Multiple ebook formats, DRM FREE
- Participation in the O'Reilly community
- Newsletters
- Account management
- 100% Satisfaction Guarantee

Signing up is easy:

1. **Go to: oreilly.com/go/register**
2. **Create an O'Reilly login.**
3. **Provide your address.**
4. **Register your books.**

Note: English-language books only

To order books online:
oreilly.com/store

For questions about products or an order:
orders@oreilly.com

To sign up to get topic-specific email announcements and/or news about upcoming books, conferences, special offers, and new technologies:
elists@oreilly.com

For technical questions about book content:
booktech@oreilly.com

To submit new book proposals to our editors:
proposals@oreilly.com

O'Reilly books are available in multiple DRM-free ebook formats. For more information:
oreilly.com/ebooks

O'REILLY®

Spreading the knowledge of innovators | oreilly.com

The information you need, when and where you need it.

With Safari Books Online, you can:

Access the contents of thousands of technology and business books

- Quickly search over 7000 books and certification guides
- Download whole books or chapters in PDF format, at no extra cost, to print or read on the go
- Copy and paste code
- Save up to 35% on O'Reilly print books
- **New!** Access mobile-friendly books directly from cell phones and mobile devices

Stay up-to-date on emerging topics before the books are published

- Get on-demand access to evolving manuscripts.
- Interact directly with authors of upcoming books

Explore thousands of hours of video on technology and design topics

- Learn from expert video tutorials
- Watch and replay recorded conference sessions

Spreading the knowledge of innovators   safari.oreilly.com

CPSIA information can be obtained at www.ICGtesting.com
Printed in the USA
269252BV00003B/2/P